*Path of*
# Wisdom,
*Path of*
# Peace

HIS HOLINESS
# THE DALAI LAMA

*Path of*
*Wisdom,*
*Path of*
*Peace*

A PERSONAL CONVERSATION

FELIZITAS VON SCHÖNBORN

Foreword by Wei Jingsheng

*A Crossroad Book*
The Crossroad Publishing Company
New York

The Crossroad Publishing Company
16 Penn Plaza, 481 Eighth Avenue
New York, NY 10001

This book was first published in 1994 by Verlag Herder in Freiburg/
Breisgau, Germany. For the second expanded edition, the author had
additional conversations with the Dalai Lama and updated the text. It was
first published in this form in 2002 by edition q of the Quintessenz
Verlags-GmbH, Berlin. Reprinted with permission.

Copyright © 2004 by Diogenes Verlag AG, Zurich, Switzerland

Translated by Christine M. Grimm. English translation copyright © 2005
by The Crossroad Publishing Company

Printed in the United States of America

This text of this book is set in 10.5/14 Goudy Old Style.
The display fonts are Liberty, News Gothic Condensed, and Zapf Chancery.


Cataloging-in-Publication Data is available from the Library of Congress
ISBN 0-8245-2311-3


1   2   3   4   5   6   7   8   9   10          10   09   08   07   06   05

# Contents

# Foreword

Describing the Dalai Lama in all his significance is an almost impossible endeavor. This book of conversations is important because in it he has the opportunity to speak about his life, Tibetan Buddhism, the dialogue of Buddhism with the modern world, the religious freedom of Tibet, the relationship between politics and religion, the spiritual crisis brought about by affluence, and various ideas of happiness. The international importance of the Dalai Lama is phenomenal. As the religious and political leader of the Tibetans, he dedicates everything he does solely to the welfare of his people. It would take many thousands of pages to fully describe his many-faceted character.

Although we had already been in contact for many years, I was not able to meet the Dalai Lama in person until three years ago. We had a wonderful understanding right from the very start, as if we were old acquaintances. Since then, a friendship has developed between us. What impresses me most is the depth of his wisdom. More than almost anyone else, he exemplifies the old Chinese proverb that highly enlightened beings often present themselves in an inconspicuous and almost simple way in public. His humility and modesty, his childlike cheerfulness and openness sometimes lead people to underestimate what an extraordinary human being the Dalai Lama is. Although he grew up isolated from the outside world in the Potala Palace, he is astonishingly capable of empathizing with the blows of fate suffered by ordinary people.

Even during our first encounter, we spoke about how much the Tibetans and the Han Chinese suffer as a result of the Chinese Communist oppressors. Yet the great compassion of the Dalai Lama extends to the plight of all oppressed peoples throughout the world. He is committed to the liberation of all people who are deprived of their rights by totalitarian states. This is more than just detached tolerance.

I would like to express my reverence here for the Dalai Lama as an enlightened being with immense farsightedness, exemplary virtue, and great wisdom.

*Wei Jingsheng*

*New York*

# Introduction

## ❀ The Dalai Lama Practices What He Preaches

Whether in Paris, Vienna, London, or Zurich, when the Dalai Lama comes, the people flock to him. Even though the motives of the listeners may vary, each of them can take home something from his words of wisdom and compassion. He presents them in a clear, understandable, and humorous way. Like almost no other person, the Fourteenth Dalai Lama embodies Eastern wisdom and the Buddhist perspective for a huge public. In an age obsessed with stars and sensations, true role models are lacking — genuine identification figures, as the psychologists say. The religious leader of the Tibetans lives what he teaches. People feel this. "Avoid all evil, do good, and purify your own heart: this is the teaching of the Buddha."

He has traveled to all parts of the earth, met with leading politicians and other important personalities as well as very simple people, and has come to the conclusion time and again that humanity is basically one big family. An old dream? An unrealizable utopia? For the Dalai Lama, this perspective has already become a question of survival because of the growing international network and the global threats to humanity. The often quoted words of Rudyard Kipling, "East is East, and West is West, and ne'er the twain shall meet," have been refuted by the Dalai Lama.

The concept of peaceful interaction with each other, so he teaches, is based on a simple fact: even though the cultural differences may be significant and manifold, we are still all mortal human beings, we long for happiness, and we want to avoid unpleasant experiences and suffering.

We are all subject to, as the French so aptly say, the *condition humaine,* the human condition of existence. The Dalai Lama's words are not those of politician concerned with reelection or of a zealous missionary, but rather of an ambassador for the Golden Rule of humanity. His message calls us to morally correct behavior toward each other: "Do unto others as you would have them do unto you." The Buddhist precepts are guidelines for a lifestyle that should fulfill everyone, a Middle Way that tries to avoid all types of extremes, a mixture of openness and suspicion.

There is a buzzing like in a beehive in the large hall of a hotel in Geneva. Small talk in many languages accompanies the aperitif. Hundreds of invited guests have gathered to listen to the words of His Holiness the Fourteenth Dalai Lama during lunch. An American woman comments loudly: "The Dalai Lama . . . he is such a funny little guy." She reports on how he supposedly sparkles with a joy for life, constantly tells jokes, and can laugh at himself. After several speeches with beautiful but empty words, a sleepiness spreads through the room. But everyone is suddenly wide awake as the "Buddhist humanist," as he calls himself, begins to speak. What he says and how he says it touches the people.

## ❀ Gandhi and the Different Glasses

In the autumn of 1988, when I met the Dalai Lama for the first time on the occasion of a meeting at the World Council of Churches, Tibetans from many parts of Switzerland were patiently waiting in front of the entrance hall for their spiritual and religious leader, the embodiment of the Bodhisattva Chenresig. Finally the Dalai Lama appeared with firm steps in his pomegranate-red and saffron-yellow robes. Red is the color of compassion, and yellow is the color of wisdom. The Tibetans threw themselves flat on the ground. In a flash, the approximately fifty-year-old monk bent down and helped the young Buddhists get back up again. This gesture left an indelible impression on me. It expressed a humble modesty, agile determination, and loving affection.

In front of the press, he knowledgeably responded to questions about the latest developments in the Chinese forced settlement of Tibet and about the suffering of his oppressed people. The Dalai Lama says that he is "a politician against his own will." And yet, it is primarily due to his personality that the drama of the Tibetans on the "Roof of the World," in the snowy land in the Himalayas, has not been completely forgotten by the international community. Even when the cameras are flashing, his humor does not desert him. In response to the question of what makes him different from Mahatma Gandhi, he responds mischievously: "We wear different glasses." And when people ask for details about his "enlightenment," he tends to quote a Tibetan saying with an amused smile: "All 'enlightened beings' are full of knowledge, but they don't have the faintest idea about anything." It is part of his Buddhist philosophy of life that this world, this valley of suffering that we must overcome, should also be a place of laughter and joy.

The president of neutral Switzerland received the Dalai Lama in Bern in August 1991 for the first time. By then, as in many countries, diplomatic recognition of China had been established — above all, for economic reasons. The Dalai Lama thanked the Swiss citizens for their reception and politely apologized for any difficulties that could arise for their country as a result. He has repeatedly come to Switzerland since 1985 because the largest Tibetan colony outside of Asia, with about two thousand members, lives here. The Dalai Lama has the type of love, kindness, and understanding that also includes political opponents.

Even when describing the cruel violations of human rights committed against his people, he — a proponent of non-violence — distances himself from any hatred toward the Chinese.

This attitude completely distinguishes the religious leader of the Tibetans from the religious fanaticism with which the Wahhabitic sect of the Taliban in Afghanistan, for example, preaches hatred and practices murderous retaliation. Christian liberation theology also moves within a delicate field of tension, especially in Latin America. On the one hand, through its silence about the deplorable state of social circumstances, the church is in danger of becoming an accomplice of the ruling classes, which frequently maintain their power only through death squads. On the other hand, liberation theologians have sometimes even taken up weapons in their commitment to the oppressed rural populations and have themselves ended up in a maelstrom of violence and counterviolence.

## A Cheerful Philosopher and the Valley of Suffering

At a church service in Zurich August 1991, during the international festival celebrating the seven-hundred-year anniversary of Switzerland, the Dalai Lama sang an old Buddhist song at the top of his lungs. Although more than

two thousand people were present, it was his personality
that permeated the large room most intensely. Next to
him, the well-known Catholic dissident Eugen Drewer-
mann of Paderborn appeared quite pale and depressed.
Like Democritus, the great Greek thinker, the Dalai Lama
is a "cheerful philosopher." He knows that true compassion
and sentimental pity are not the same thing.

In the spring of 1993, I met the Dalai Lama on the
occasion of the Vienna Human Rights Conference. The
Chinese wanted to prevent him from speaking about the
suffering of his six million people under their rule. But
this had the result of attracting even greater attention to
the cause of Tibet. How seriously the Chinese take the
Dalai Lama is shown by a statement made by Mao Zedong. When he heard of the successful flight of the Dalai
Lama in 1959, he reportedly said: "I believe that we have
lost the battle for Tibet." His evaluation of the Tibetan
people certainly was right on this point. Even today, after
more than forty years of antireligious propaganda, Tibet
is still one of the most religious countries on earth. The
Dalai Lama in exile has remained the symbolic figure of
nonviolent resistance.

During our conversations, his inimitable and conta-
gious laughter rang out time and again. A colleague once
revealed to me that she listens to this laughter on her

tape recorder whenever she is feeling gloomy. In the Viennese hotel, the monks and staff members who look after him came and went. Their reverence was tangible. The leader of the Tibetans listened to my every word. His partners in conversation are impressed again and again by his listening abilities. He responded to my questions in his stumbling English, yet still acknowledged everyone who entered the room with a nod of his head. He does not want anyone to feel left out. Awareness is an important Buddhist virtue.

## ✸ Meditation and Power Politics

He is really a very unusual human being. The Dalai Lama combines the uninhibited manner of a "divine child" with the initiative of a politician and the intellectual agility of a philosophically trained thinker. At the same time, he radiates a kindness and warm-heartedness that let every insecurity and all mistrust disappear. His language is childlike in its simplicity, sometimes even banal, and yet it causes deep levels of the soul to resonate. His daily meditation does not seem to transport him to distant spiritual worlds; instead, it gives him the strength to maintain his originality, even during the countless human encounters on his trips around the world with frequent media appearances. An unbroken wisdom that dates back thousands of years speaks through him. He embodies Tibetan Buddhism, which today is still the most intact and complete form of Buddhism in the world. Despite the intricate and complex edifice of his thoughts, everyone can follow his humane words.

Tenzin Gyatso, the Fourteenth Dalai Lama, comes from a family of farmers. He still radiates rustic strength in the best sense of the word. His education is grounded in an ancient tradition. Yet in contrast to his predecessors, he moves today on the world's political stage for the cause of the Tibetan people. He is also interested in modern technological inventions and loves to converse with Western scientists about their latest findings.

This Dalai Lama builds bridges between different worlds in a way that almost no one else does: between the origins of Buddhism more than twenty-five hundred years ago and the latest speculative theses of nuclear physicists, between the perseverance of the Far East and the hectic Western world, between religious teachings and political power interests, between meditative contemplation and active involvement in the world. Since the Nobel Peace Prize was awarded to him in 1989, he has become one of the great spiritual leaders of our day through his untiring commitment to a more humane world.

❀  Images Arising from the Lake

Time and again, people in the West are surprised to learn
how the Tibetans find their leader. In earlier times, it was
the task of the government in Lhasa to locate the new
Dalai Lama. Since every Dalai Lama is the reincarnation of
his predecessor, the search for the new incarnation doesn't
begin until some years after the death of a Dalai Lama. In
1933, when the Thirteenth Dalai Lama died, the National
Assembly appointed Reting Rinpoche to be the regent for
the interim period. Two years later, the regent went on
a pilgrimage with various other dignitaries to the sacred
Lhamoi-Lhatso Lake at the Chokhogyal Monastery, 150
kilometers (88 miles) south of Lhasa. The Tibetans say
that this lake allows the person asking a question to have
visions and insights into other worlds. Reting Rinpoche
and his entourage recognized three Tibetan letters on the
surface of the water: Ah, Ka, and Ma. Among other things,
they also saw the golden and jade-green roofs of a monastery and a small farmhouse with turquoise tiles. This vision
was kept secret at first.

The stories of the monks who wander through the distant "Land of Snow" to find the reincarnation of their
leader through signs and miracles sounds like a wondrous
fairy tale to Western ears. It reminds us of the biblical

legend of the wise men from the Orient who set out to look for the divine infant Jesus. Even today, the Dalai Lama and his government consult the Nechung Oracle about their state affairs. An oracle with its clairvoyant abilities is seen as the mediator between the natural and the spiritual realms. The current Dalai Lama, however, emphasizes that he does not personally have such abilities.

With regard to the vision of Reting Rinpoche at the sacred Lhamoi-Lhatso Lake, through whose help the Dalai Lama was found, he says in his laconic, humorous way: "That is probably an ancient form of television." But it is also true that through centuries of spiritual training the Tibetans have developed "para-psychological" technologies, which have hardly been researched by science. However, for the high lamas these are only secondary manifestations; they are primarily concerned with spiritual transformation, the main goal of which is loving-kindness toward all beings.

## Prayer Beads, Walking Staffs, and the Lama from Sera

In 1937 various search parties were sent out to look for the buildings that were seen in the sacred lake. Since the corpse of the deceased Thirteenth Dalai Lama, which was still sitting on his throne, had its face turned toward the east, the search was concentrated in this direction. Ket-sang Rinpoche from the Sera Monastery and two other monks, searching in the northeastern province of Amado in Dokham, found the Kumbum Monastery with its gold-green roofs. And in the neighboring village of Trakster, they discovered a farmhouse with turquoise tiles. Both corresponded with the vision. Before the three monks en-tered the house, Ketsang Rinpoche exchanged his clothes with those of a servant. He kept the prayer beads of the deceased Thirteenth Dalai Lama with him.

As the supposed servant sat down in the kitchen, the two-year-old Lhamo Thöndup, who was born on July 6, 1935, trustingly jumped in his lap and immediately reached for the prayer beads. The Rinpoche promised the child the rosary if he could guess the man's identity. With-out giving it any thought, the boy said: "The lama from Sera." In the same breath he added the names of the other two strangers. This was followed by a series of tests.

Genuine objects that belonged to the deceased Dalai Lama and copies that closely resembled the real ones were shown to the boy. When he was shown two black and two yellow rosaries, as well as two prayer wheels, he selected the right ones without difficulty. With the two walking sticks, the child first hesitated but then reached for the genuine one. This was considered additional proof that the boy must be the reincarnation of the Dalai Lama. The walking stick the boy selected was the one the Thirteenth Dalai Lama had always had with him; the other he had given away after a short time.

## The "Lord of the White Lotus" Ascends the Throne

It was agreed that the syllable *Ah* stood for Amado, the syllable *Ka* indicated the Kumbum Monastery, and *Ma* meant the Karma Polpai Dorje Monastery, in which the Thirteenth Dalai Lama stayed on his journey back from China. Through these and other signs, they were strengthened in the conviction that the little boy must actually be the Fourteenth Dalai Lama. However, they still faced tough negotiations with the Muslim governor who controlled the area around Trakster on behalf of the Chinese. Only after the payment of a high ransom was it possible to bring the boy, who was five years old by then, and his family to the capital city in the year 1940.

In Lhasa he received the monk's name of Tenzin Gyatso and was officially proclaimed the Fourteenth Dalai Lama. On the day of his accession to the throne, he was given additional names: "Lord of the White Lotus," "The Wish-Fulfilling Gem," "Victorious Jewel," "Incomparable Master." The Tibetans simply call their leader *Kundun*,

which means "Presence." The boy now began to follow
a path upon which he would soon encounter difficult
political tasks.

## ❀ Yellow Hats and Red Hats

To better appreciate the role of the Dalai Lama, it is important to understand some basic concepts. He is both the
spiritual and the political leader of Tibet, as well as head
of the "School of the Virtuous," the Gelugpas. Because
of their clothing, they are also called "Yellow Hats." The
head of the second main school, the "Kagyü School" or
the "Red Hats," is the Karmapa. The current Seventeenth
Karmapa is Urgyen Trinley, who was recognized in 1992
by the Dalai Lama. Late in the year of 2000, much like the
Dalai Lama in 1959, he fled from his Tibetan monastery
of Tsurphu, over the Himalayas to Dharamsala in north
India.

Both of these spiritual leaders are bodhisattvas for the
Buddhists. They are perfected "enlightened beings" who
could enter nirvana after their death but forgo it because
of compassion, *karuna*, until all other beings are liberated.
They are considered to be incarnations of the Bodhisattva
Chenresig ("Looking with Clear Eyes"), the patron saint
of the Land of Snow, Tibet. The people of Tibet link all

major occurrences and important personalities with his activities. The "Father of the Tibetan People," King Songtsen Gampo (620–649), is also seen as his embodiment. The path of a bodhisattva begins with *bodhicitta,* the spirit of enlightenment, and with a vow, *pranidhana.*

## ❀ The Protector of All Religions

Under the Dalai Lamas, Tibet developed into a hierarchic monastic state with a rich monastic culture. The Chinese Cultural Revolution has largely destroyed this. However, the Dalai Lama still remains the protector of all Buddhist traditions in Tibet, as well as the ancient native Bön religion and Islam, which is also present in the Land of Snow.

The second spiritual leader after the Dalai Lama is the Panchen Lama. He is considered to be the incarnation of the Buddha Amitabha (Amida), one of the most important and popular Buddhas. Up to now, the Panchen Lama has been the acting spiritual leader after the death of a Dalai Lama. The last Panchen Lama died suddenly in January 1989 under circumstances that still have not been clarified.

The Dalai Lama selected six-year-old Gendun Choekyi Nyima as successor to the Panchen Lama in 1995. In response, the Chinese immediately presented their own Panchen Lama. Since then, there has been no precise information about the fate of Nyima and his parents. According to Chinese rumors, he has been banished to a remote province of Tibet. The exiled Tibetans call Nyima "the youngest political prisoner in the world." Quite recently, Beijing appears to have agreed to allow spiritual dignitaries appointed by the Dalai Lama to participate in the search for the child.

When the Dalai Lama moved into the Potala Palace as a child, Ling Rinpoche and Trijang Rinpoche mainly attended to his religious education. He saw his parents, who were raised to nobility, once a month. He impressed people with his quick intellectual grasp. Heinrich Harrer reported that the young Dalai Lama was already a remarkably independent youth. As a result, he was a sharp contrast to many of his predecessors, who spent their entire lifetimes as puppets in the hands of their mentors and left the government to regents.

Harrer, who also taught the Dalai Lama and made him known in Europe through his popular book *Seven Years in Tibet*, wrote: "Even now, people say wondrous things about the intelligence of this boy. They say that he only needs to read a book once to memorize it. At an early age, he was already interested in all the matters of state and criticized or praised the decisions of the National Assembly." As early as the age of fifteen, the Dalai Lama began his public religious teachings.

## ✿ Head of State in the Young Years

When Tibet was threatened by Communist China, the Dalai Lama, at the age of sixteen, assumed political responsibility. Like his predecessors, he attempted to democratize the strict theocratic order of Tibet. However, he met with great resistance in the process. He wanted to eliminate the principle of inherited debt that doomed many families to lasting poverty. This displeased the Tibetan elite, who feared they would lose their privileges. He was also actively committed to a system of universal education. For the Chinese occupiers, a Dalai Lama as a reformer did not fit into their concepts of feudalism, from which they wanted to "liberate" the Tibetans.

In a certain sense, he stumbled into world politics and became a politician against his will. The Chinese increasingly limited the initially granted autonomy of the Dalai Lama. In 1954, together with the Panchen Lama, he attempted in vain to negotiate with Mao Zedong and Zhou Enlai in Beijing on the freedom of Tibet. In 1956, he met with Prime Minister Pandit Nehru in India; Nehru received him only as a religious leader and did not help him. As the situation of the Tibetans continually worsened under the Chinese, the Dalai Llama fled into Indian exile in 1959 with almost a hundred thousand Tibetans and created an exile government. From then on, his main task has been to make it easier for the many refugees who have followed their leader to resettle in India.

In 1963, he drafted a constitution that was designed to make it possible for the Tibetan people to be governed democratically in the future. The world hardly noticed the exile government at that time — although there were three unfruitful UN resolutions that addressed its status. Like Nehru, many Western political leaders received the Dalai Lama only as a religious leader and not as a head of state. After the acceptance of the People's Republic of China into the United Nations, the question of the exiled government was not discussed until 1991. Economic considerations were in the foreground. States that wanted to do business with the Chinese were afraid of annoying China by mentioning its violations of human rights. At the Human Rights Conference in June 1993 in Vienna, China initially succeeded in excluding the Dalai Lama. The ban on his participation was lifted only when the Austrian foreign minister, Alois Mock, intervened in his position as president of this UN conference.

On the occasion of his twenty-second visit to Germany in 1999, the Dalai Lama was received by both Foreign Minister Joschka Fischer and Minister of the Interior Otto Schily. During these visits, the Dalai Lama pleaded for the true cultural autonomy of Tibet and for a solution mutually acceptable to Tibet and Beijing. The German federal government let it be known that it did not support the independence of Tibet but adhered to its one-China policy.

The "Millennium World Summit" in New York in August 2000 was also shadowed by the absence of the Dalai Lama — for which the People's Republic of China was responsible. More than a thousand spiritual leaders of all religions met for a four-day summit on world peace. They wanted to reduce faith-related tensions and show their commitment to peace, protection of the environment, and the battle against poverty. As a compromise solution, the organizers of the summit finally suggested that the second part of the conference be moved to New York's Waldorf Astoria Hotel. The Dalai Lama was invited to speak the closing words of the conference. The Tibetan leader, however, refused this invitation with the official statement that he did not want to become the reason for differences.

In 1990, after the Czechoslovakian president, Vaclav Havel, received the Dalai Lama — as did the pope and

President Carlos Santos of Mexico — the ice appeared to have been broken. This was followed in 1991 by visits with George H. W. Bush, English prime minister John Major, and Norwegian prime minister Gro Harlem Brundtland. He visited Bill Clinton and Thomas Klestil in 1993 and Nelson Mandela in 1996. In 1998, he was at the Elysée Palace with Jacques Chirac and Lionel Jospin. In his untiring commitment to the cause of Tibet, the Dalai Lama has traveled to fifty-two countries. In addition to winning the Nobel Peace Prize in 1989, His Holiness wears twenty-six honorary doctorate hats, holds honorary professorships at two Russian universities, and has written more than fifty books. Yet his government has not been recognized by any state up to now.

The institution of the Dalai Lama has become controversial among Tibetans. For example, By Huitzi wrote in the magazine for the exiled Tibetans *Lungta* (no. 7) that the devout conduct of many Tibetans toward the Dalai Lama makes the "process of democratization" more difficult for the exiled community. They still think of him as the indisputable master, so that those who criticize the leader are placing themselves above him. At the same time, the Dalai Lama himself is a prisoner of the monastic tradition, which he cannot question. But those are merely isolated voices among Tibetans abroad.

## ❀ From Potala to Dharamsala

His Holiness the Fourteenth Dalai Lama does not live like his predecessors, shielded from the rest of the world in the gigantic Potala Palace, the winter residence of previous Dalai Lamas in the Tibetan capital city of Lhasa. The palace, with more than a thousand rooms and halls, with a school for public officials, a monastery, and many temples, was a symbol of the hierarchic position of the spiritual and political leader of the Tibetans. "Up to that time, we were frozen in formalities," he says in retrospect. "We could hardly speak freely or breathe. In a certain respect, the flight from Lhasa was very healing. In addition, I gained an even deeper understanding of religion as a result, especially in the sense of the impermanence of all things."

Since his flight, the Dalai Lama has lived a simple monk's life in Indian Dharamsala and never stopped working for his people with an untiring commitment. In his lectures on harmony and world peace, he strives for a better understanding between religions and cultures. His thoughts can be understood by everyone. The Dalai Lama urgently calls for an attitude of universal responsibility in order to overcome the global dangers to humanity. The message is that each of us should empathize with the suffering and needs of others and make them our own. His universal Buddhist perspective crosses all borders and barriers.

The following conversations took place during a number of encounters in Switzerland and Austria between the years 1988 and 1993. In various places, it has been supplemented and revised for the sake of clarity. It was often necessary to bridge the language barriers with a translation from Tibetan. Despite this, I hope that I have succeeded in reproducing something of the Fourteenth Dalai Lama's complex simplicity.

I would like to thank Tica Broch and Arianne Poux in Geneva, the representatives of the Tibet Support Committee in Switzerland, Gyaltsen Gyaltag in Zurich, the representatives of the Dalai Lama in Central and Southern Europe, as well as at the UN and the EU, Geshe Thupten Tinpa in Dharamsala, Lama Tchokdroup, Gonsar Rinpoche, the abbot of Mont Pèlerin, Alexandra Hohenlohe and Anja Meran, as well as Lea Spier, Dr. Wan-Hussan Yao-Weyrauch, and Shan-Shan Wei-Blank for their help and support.

# Conversation

# About the Person

### ✺ A Human Being Like Everyone Else

> FVS: *Even people who know hardly anything about Buddhism or Tibet pay attention when they hear the words "Dalai Lama." For many people the sound evokes the snow-covered mountains of Tibet with colorfully dressed inhabitants and artistic tankas. What does the office of the Dalai Lama mean to you personally?*

His Holiness: As you can imagine, there are high expectations of the Dalai Lama everywhere, and many people respect me. But I am a human being like everyone else. I am a monk who should be more concerned about others than about myself. Every day I try with all my might to work on perfecting myself. We call this *bodhicitta*, the mind of enlightenment. This is the altruistic desire to attain enlightenment in order to free all sentient beings from their suffering. In a prayer from the eighth century, this desire is expressed in these words:

As long as space and time exist, as long as there are still beings who must wander through the cycle of rebirth time and again, may I also be with them and take the suffering from them.

In Tibetan Buddhism, we believe that the Dalai Lama is an incarnation of Avalokiteshvara (*Chenresig* in Tibetan). He is the bodhisattva of mercy and the protector of all living beings. I am the seventy-fourth incarnation, which can be followed back to a Brahman boy at the time of the Buddha Sakyamuni. We believe in beings, great lamas or *tulkus* (as they are called in Tibetan), who can determine their rebirth on their own. These lamas include the Dalai Lama, whose reincarnation had its origins in 1351. These reincarnations take place only so that the Dalai Lamas can continue to fulfill their tasks. This is a significant factor in the search for the respective successor. According to our beliefs, there is a spiritual connection and a karmic force that enables me to assume the role of the Dalai Lama.

## An Ocean of Wisdom

*What do the words "Dalai Lama" mean?*

*Lama* means "the Unsurpassable Master." *Dalai* is a Mongolian word that means something like "Ocean." In the figurative sense, Dalai Lama means an "Ocean of Wisdom." I believe, however, that the title is related to the Third Dalai Lama, Sonam Gyatso. According to tradition, he was first given the title of Dalai by a Mongolian chieftain. It may well be that the word *Gyatso*, which means "ocean" in Tibetan, was translated into the Mongolian language. Until the fifth reincarnation, the Dalai Lamas had only religious functions. The Fifth Dalai Lama was the first to assume the leadership of the state as well, so that political and religious leadership became unified in one person.

## ❊ *Helping Others Is the Meaning of My Existence*

*In Europe, it appears that the spiritual and the worldly forces have never truly succeeded in working together in harmony. How was it possible in Tibet to unite in one person two opposing ways of being — the simplicity of a mendicant and the political activity of the head of a state?*

Whether as a monk or as the head of state, for me the meaning of life is to help others — especially the six million Tibetans who place all their hopes in me. As a result,

I carry considerable responsibility on my shoulders. Of course, I primarily see my mission as helping my people and serving them with my total dedication. When we sincerely help others, we benefit doubly because at the same time we make ourselves happy.

How I do justice to my role largely depends on me. Only when I succeed in truly fulfilling my mission does the office of the Dalai Lama become something useful. But for me, my personal integrity and the authenticity of my motivation are certainly what is decisive — separately from whether or not I as a politician can achieve the goals of my people.

On the other hand, obviously, it is also dangerous if the Tibetan people expect that the oppressive circumstances in our homeland can be changed by a single person, even if that person is the Dalai Lama. This is not just about today; we must also find solutions for the welfare and survival of our nation in future generations. This is my main concern.

Originally I was not at all prepared for this task in world politics. When I took over the government in 1950 at the age of sixteen, I completely lacked political experience. I could hardly deal with the diplomatic practices. This has changed in the meantime. I've benefited from my experiences over the decades and my numerous contacts with political leaders and other important figures.

## ✤ My Great School Was Life Itself

*Your Holiness, you said that you were inadequately pre-pared for the important role you play in world politics today. Is there a special education for the Dalai Lama?*

I did not have any other type of training than what is customary for Tibetan monks. At the age of thirteen I began to study philosophy, the proper defining of terms, and the art of debate. Then the art of calligraphy. After writing lessons, I had to memorize Buddhist texts. My curriculum consisted of five major and five minor subjects. The major subjects were dialectics, Tibetan art and culture, grammar and linguistics, medicine, and Buddhist philosophy. The five minor subjects were poetry, music and drama, astrology, metrics and expression, and vocabulary. The doctorate required Buddhist philosophy, logic and dialectics, and epistemology. In 1959 while I was still in Tibet, shortly before my flight into Indian exile, I completed my studies with an exam — a disputation in front of thousands of people. I had the title of *Geshe* conferred upon me, the highest philosophical degree.

I also gained many insights by meditating several times a day on a regular basis. We have two main types of meditation. One focuses on concentration, inner peace; the other involves analysis, deeper insight into things. In my own meditation practice I am mainly concerned with compassion, with the differentiation between the self and others and with the way all things and living beings, especially human beings, are interdependent on each other. I pray, meditate, or study every day for at least five and a half hours. I also pray during the rest of the day whenever I get the chance. We have prayers for everything that we do. For Buddhists, there is hardly any distinction between religion and everyday life.

My most important school was life itself, with its enormous challenges and the many difficulties that my people have to face. My fate as a refugee has frequently brought me into desperate, almost hopeless situations. It has constantly forced me to confront naked reality. Under this constant pressure, I time and again have had to prove my outer decisiveness and my inner strength. This was above all about not losing courage and hope. The daily meditation and my life experience are the two areas to which I probably owe the greatest debt.

## ✸ The Clocks Ticked Differently
## in the Potala Palace

*As a child in the gigantic Potala Palace, separated from your family, weren't you very secluded from the rest of the world?*

The protocol for the life of a Dalai Lama was very strict at that time. My life was characterized by routine. I cannot remember the precise hourly schedule, however, because at that time Tibetans did not place much importance on living according to the clock. Things started and ended as they happened in the moment and without any haste. In this respect I was an exception because as a child I was already interested in clocks. Repairing clock mechanisms is still one of my favorite activities.

Even as a child, I didn't care for formalities. I was especially close to the kitchen manager. From my servants, who treated me like any other little boy, I already learned quite early that life could be difficult for common folk. They told me that there were unjust high government officials and lamas who often made very arbitrary decisions. At a young age, I recognized that the leader of a people needs to be connected with common folk. It is easy to be persuaded by advisers and officials into making decisions that are in their own interests. Along the way, the genuine concerns of the people can be overlooked.

## 🏵 *The White Lotus Grows in the Mud*

*You said that the Dalai Lama is the reincarnation of a bodhisattva. Could you please explain what this means in Tibetan Buddhism?*

For us, a bodhisattva is a "being of enlightenment" who forgoes Buddhahood, meaning complete enlightenment, out of compassion for all other beings until he has helped liberate them. A bodhisattva reincarnates at his own wish. So he voluntarily decides to remain in the cycle of rebirth, in samsara, to help others. He wants to take on the suffering of others in their place. This is called the "practice of giving and taking," in which the suffering of others is taken on and one's own happiness is given back to them.

A symbol for the way in which the bodhisattva has overcome the desires and passions of life is the lotus blossom. This very beautiful flower grows in the mud, yet its white color remains unscathed by the dirt. A power that makes us resistant to the chaos of becoming and dying grows out of this. "Bodhi" means understanding the actual nature of reality or wisdom, and a "sattva" is someone who acts out of all-encompassing compassion. According to the bodhisattva ideal, we should strive to practice never-ending compassion with infinite wisdom.

My path is that of a monk. This means that I follow the 235 vows for a monk. The four main vows prohibit a monk from killing, stealing, and lying about his spiritual knowledge. A monk must also strictly keep the vow of chastity. These rules free me from many distractions and worries of everyday life.

## A Smile Is More Beautiful Than Jewels

*We often see pictures of Tibetan lamas dressed in magnificent silk robes. Is there a reason why Your Holiness is always dressed very simply?*

I wear the robes that are customary for a Tibetan monk. In keeping with tradition, this consists of different pieces and is intended to remind us of patched garments and so symbolize poverty.

This clothing has absolutely no meaning in terms of spiritual development, however. In the Tibetan tradition, the great lamas are often dressed quite splendidly. They wear various hats differentiated by shape and color in keeping with their office. Whenever I meet a Lama dressed in this way, I admonish him: "Our true master is the Buddha, and he did not own a hat. We are just students. The Buddha had a much greater right than we to dress luxuriously because he is the true master. Yet he still preferred to remain a simple monk." Anyone can dress extravagantly or hang jewels on himself. But it is an illusion to believe that this will change something essential in a human being. Compassion and love, a heartfelt smile, a kind look — I believe this is the most valuable jewelry there is. An unfriendly face does not become more beautiful, even with the most ornate decoration.

Sometimes I also think that if I always walked around with a grim face and did not smile as much, there would be fewer friends interested in the cause of Tibet. So I engage in the politics of the smile.

## ❀ *A Free Tibet Will Vote on Its Own*

*Your Holiness, because you no longer consider the Tibetan social system appropriate for our day, the first thing you did when you drafted the constitution in 1963 was to restrict the power of the Dalai Lama. And you said in your 1988 speech in Strasbourg that you would not want to play an active role in a new government of*

*Tibet. Will the Dalai Lama be only the spiritual head of Tibet from now on?*

I will do whatever is best for my people. I have decided that I will hand over the role of political leader in a free Tibet. Then I will be just the spiritual head. After all, the Dalai Lamas originally only had religious tasks to fulfill. I will transfer my political office to a Tibetan elected by the people.

## No Return Yet to Lhasa

*Under what conditions would the Dalai Lama return to Tibet?*

The majority of Tibetans who live in Tibet — especially the young people — think that I should not return at this time because I can represent the cause of Tibet much more effectively from abroad. The most important precondition for my return is that the Chinese accept my suggestions and that the people in Tibet are truly satisfied with the political situation.

## Pilgrims Bring the News

*Is there someone who represents Your Holiness in Tibet?*

In Tibet itself there is no one. There is only an indirect exchange through the Tibetans who come to India on pilgrimages and then go back again. Or through people who are allowed to visit their relatives in Tibet. A great deal of information flows to Tibet through such contacts. Of course, the media also helps us. There is a Tibetan program in Indian broadcasting, and also one on the Voice of America.

## ❀ A New Dalai Lama Will Appear When the World Needs Him

*Will there be a fifteenth incarnation of the Dalai Lama? Your Holiness once said that you may possibly be the last Dalai Lama.*

This statement must be understood in connection with the unreasonable ideas of the Chinese who want to define the Tibet issue solely as the problem of the Dalai Lama and the Tibetans in exile. We have no intention of reintroducing the old feudal system. Even if we had, it would be impossible and inappropriate for our times. This form of government would certainly no longer benefit the people. If the Tibetan people of today believed that they could do without the institution of the Dalai Lama, then that

would be the end of this office, and I would be the last
Dalai Lama. A new Dalai Lama will appear when the circumstances call for him. But if history takes a different
course, we must also accept this. Political systems change;
the only thing that never changes is the human heart, the
longing for happiness, the striving for freedom. These are
the true reasons for continued development and progress,
whether in the material realm or the spiritual. This is also
true for my Tibetan people.

# About Tibetan Buddhism

※ ## Even If the Monks Dress Differently, the Four Noble Truths Still Apply

*The lamas play an essential role in Tibetan Buddhism. Is it therefore correct to consider it to be "Lamaism," with a lineage separate from the original Indian Buddhism?*

Anyone familiar with Tibetan Buddhism knows that there is no reason to speak of it as a different school from Indian Buddhism. So even if the Tibetan monks and nuns look different from the Indians externally, in their clothing, we do follow the ancient Indian texts in all of the important respects. The heart of Buddhist practice is to harm no one and to help others according to the best of our abilities. We Tibetans live according to Mahayana Buddhism, the "Greater Vehicle," as it is called. For us, what's decisive is self-sacrifice and altruism, and that our thoughts and our actions are always focused upon the welfare of others. By way of comparison, the primary striving of the older Hinayana, the "Lesser Vehicle," is not to harm anyone.

## ❀ A Different Way of Thinking without Fighting

*Different schools and currents have developed in Maha-
yana Buddhism. In contrast to the West, why haven't
these different teachings led to divisions? Is it still possible for monks of various philosophical schools to live
together in a single monastery?*

Buddhism came to Tibet gradually and through different
teachers. So various traditions developed. Although there
are major philosophical differences between these schools,
we all agree on the cardinal points. Like anywhere else,
people here also express their opinions in different ways.

## ❀ Even the Common People Love a Sharp Debate

*Buddhist training includes debating. Is it perhaps eas-
ier for different schools to live together peacefully when
the philosophical debates take place according to specific
rules, almost like a ritual?*

That may be. The intellectual abilities of a monk are
judged according to how well he can prove himself in the
art of debating. This occurs in this way: Two monks ask
each other questions. As they do this, they must carry out
very specific physical movements. The challenger claps

his hand and stamps on the floor with his foot, as if he wants the battle to begin. The debate can become very heated. Each relentlessly tries to disprove all the opponent's arguments. This is a matter of being quick-witted, ingenious, and witty. For us, philosophical or religious discussions are not a reason for personal conflict. When the monks leave the "arena" after a hard battle of words, they are not angry at each other. In earlier times, these debates were also very popular with the common Tibetans. They would sit for hours in the inner courts of the monastery as listeners and delight in the sharp debates, although they certainly did not understand much of the intellectual hair-splitting.

## ✺ A Religion without God

*For Christians, a religion like Buddhism that does not recognize a Creator God is an atheistic religion and a contradiction in itself. If I understand it correctly, however, Tibetan Buddhism avoids both the belief in the one God and the unbelief?*

There are two types of religions. The first type, such as Buddhism or Jainism, are religions without a personal God. Then there are the monotheistic religions such as Judaism,

Christianity, and Islam, which believe in a creator of the world. The creation of the world, the causes and effects of happiness and suffering, are explained by these religions in different ways.

Buddhism is atheistic because we do not believe in a Creator God. But we do recognize higher beings who have passed through a process of purification. Every sentient being bears within itself the potential to attain this spiritual realization or high spiritual level. We also assume that there are different levels of existence. This is where the major world religions differ from one another.

Buddhism is based on the Four Noble Truths. We Buddhists live in a world without a god. For many of the others, the Creator God is the center of doctrine. But they all agree that love and compassion make people better. For our religion, *mahakaruna*, the great healing kindness toward all sentient beings, is the most important thing.

## ❀ *The Buddha's Teachings Are Logical*

*If there is no personal God, to whom do you pray?*

In the monotheistic religions, the believers hope for God's help in order to master the difficulties of their existence.

This concept of the omnipotence of God gives no answer to the question of why an omnipotent and kind God has also created suffering and injustice. We could even imagine this God to be cruel because he lets people come into a world where they experience suffering and pain. But the Buddha was concerned with giving logical reasons for everything he taught. The Creation, the beginning of all things, has nothing to do with logic. Religions that have the concept of such a God prohibit their followers from questioning the "Word of God" or even rejecting it — even if it should contradict their critical common sense. This gives rise to the danger that believers subject themselves to God's commandments only out of blind obedience. We think that blind belief does not lead us any further on the path of enlightenment.

For us, the focus is not on God but on enlightenment. Human beings are responsible for their own lives. We alone are the creators of our fate. The Buddha did not create the world, nor is he responsible for its deficiencies. But he shows us ways in which we can move from the present state of suffering to perfection. Because of this and other reasons, the Buddha did not address teachings about the existence of God.

❀ *The One and the Other Self*

> *There are essential differences not only in the concept of God but also in the human image. An independent self, as we know it, does not appear to exist for Buddhists. For them, the self consists of suffering. Today, analytic psychology in particular emphasizes the importance of a strong self. How do you explain such fundamentally different ways of thinking?*

Our body knows what it desires: if it is thirsty, then we drink. The Buddha called all desires thirst. For him, thirst is the force that drives the cycle of existence. And yet, without this thirst we could not attain liberation, Buddhahood. But even on the level of body consciousness we must recognize differences, because the body can also desire harmful things. It can become addicted to luxury items and destroy itself.

All things have two sides. This is true of the human self as well. There is the egotistical self that constantly inflates itself and becomes a disastrous troublemaker. And when individuals inconsiderately assert themselves because of ego addiction, they hurt not only others but themselves. This self causes suffering. Then there is the self of the will, which lets people say: "I can, I must, I want."

When this center of the will is lacking, a person cannot deal with negative aspects, such as anger, envy, or hatred, and instead is overwhelmed by them. Our sensations and feelings react spontaneously. We want to possess something or we reject it. Only a strongly developed will can manage the various feelings.

❀ ## There Are Medicinal Herbs and Poisonous Herbs

*We must constantly choose, but our feelings are in conflict.*

True. An example of this is self-confidence and pride. Both are related to our own self-esteem. Pride can make us overbearing, conceited, and inconsiderate, but without self-confidence we can hardly achieve anything. Humility can be pathological shyness, the feeling of helplessness, or it can be a magnanimous service to others, the courage to serve. Anger can often make us violent, but we can also become incensed about injustice and then stand take a stand for justice.

When I was young, I became angry easily. This may run in my family, because my father had a similar temperament. But today it is possible for me to control my fits of anger through spiritual mental exercises. We should not stop exercising our mind, because that is the only way for the intellect to differentiate between what is beneficial for it and what harms it. In order to strengthen this attitude within myself, I visualize the following image time and again: I am standing alone, and facing me is a large crowd of people. And I ask myself: Whose interests are more important? My own, or those of the countless other people?

Feelings are like plants or fruits. Some are very beneficial for people, but others are poisonous and should be avoided. I recently visited the Holocaust Museum in Washington. For me, it was a symbol of what people are capable of, in both the good and the bad sense. Here were horrible pictures showing the tribulation of the Jewish people, and there were pictures of people who sacrificed their lives to save others.

Even love and hatred appear to be similar to each other, and yet they have such different effects. Loving desire often changes into its opposite and becomes consuming hatred. Hatred is always harmful and drives people to commit the worst atrocities. We have the free will to decide whether we want to hate or love.

## Mahakaruna

*Can we compare Mahakaruna, great loving-kindness to all sentient beings and the main element of Tibetan Mahayana Buddhism, with Christian brotherly love, of which it is written in 1 Corinthians: "Love does not insist on its own way, it is not irritable or resentful . . . it rejoices in the truth . . . "?*

That is difficult to say. Perhaps they are different in that *mahakaruna* is compassion but not sympathy. I don't know whether this distinction also exists in Christianity. If we pity another person, it can easily happen that we look down upon the other's life and fate. We certainly do not want this to happen. From the Buddhist perspective loving-kindness says that we truly take the other person seriously. The love must also be uninhibited and must not stop with the sympathy that we feel for our friends or our own family. It must include our enemies.

## The Love That Excludes No One

*In my native language of German, the word "love" includes a broad spectrum of feelings. In any case, we think of a heartfelt and strong feeling of affection. The form of love that you are speaking about is also based on clearer insight. It also includes people that we do not find likeable.*

Genuine love, as I have said, does not depend on a special relationship. It does not need a personal bond. This is why we must learn not to confuse feelings of affection or falling in love with true love. All too often, friendliness toward our fellow humans disappears when personal affection disappears. In that case we are nice to someone only as long as we like that person.

*Mahakaruna*, great loving-kindness toward all beings, is the basic attitude of Mahayana Buddhism. For us, it is the most precious thing. We say that it will exist as long as there are suffering beings. We can let our compassion become greater and greater because there are no boundaries to loving-kindness. The belief in reincarnation is important for this way of thinking because in the wheel of rebirth, in the eternal cycle, all beings become mother and father to each other.

❀ *Return of the Enlightened One*

*The teaching of reincarnation of all beings is not in harmony with the Christian tradition, because we see "life in Christ" as the ultimate goal. Yet many Europeans, one in every four according to some surveys, believe in rebirth. . . .*

How we are born into the next life depends on our mental attitude in the present life. We believe in four types of rebirth. In general, it is not in our power to choose under what circumstances we are reincarnated. Our state during the dying process has an influence upon which karmic dispositions are in effect. On the lowest level, a reincarnation is determined completely by the actions in one's previous life. On the next level, it is possible to have some influence on the choice of the place or the surroundings of the new life. On a third level there are people who are especially qualified to act as religious teachers or masters. On the last level is the completely enlightened Buddha, who is reincarnated only in order to assist others.

According to Tibetan tradition, we believe that we should not use up the fruits of previous lives in our existence as humans, as spiritual beings. This means that if we have accumulated good karma in a previous existence through good deeds and a proper lifestyle, then we should not use this up now by living a life of luxury. We also should not sit back and rest on the laurels of our good deeds but look ahead and strive for even greater perfection. For us, human life itself is something very valuable and a great opportunity on the path of perfection.

## ✤ *Now Is the Time to Do Good*

> *The goal of perfection is nirvana, the "extinguishing" of all suffering....*

Our existence from birth to death is full of suffering. The goal of our religious striving must be to end the suffering. Anyone who overcomes suffering in this world (*dukha*) has entered into the state of liberation. Suffering does not just mean the things that are unpleasant, but life itself, which is subject to eternal becoming, to creation and dissolution. Nirvana is the ultimate goal that is difficult to achieve, the attainment of a state of complete peace. This should allow our compassion for other people to grow more and more in order to help them.

## ✤ *This Is Not about Material Dreams*

> *So Buddhism is concerned with bringing the sorrowful "Wheel of Rebirth" to a halt. A Westernized approach to the teachings of reincarnation hopes that through better*

*rebirths we come closer and closer to self-realization. People hope that every new life will bring a better form of existence.*

What do people understand a good life to be ? It cannot be equated with a pleasant life in which all of our material wishes and dreams are fulfilled. Instead, it is a life lived in ethical responsibility. A life in which we do not think only of our own well-being but also serve others. Good karma is created only through good deeds. As a result of doing good, we become better persons and find a truly superior place in this life and the next life. We reach a higher level on the path to nirvana. Every soul is the continuation of an earlier soul. We base the belief in rebirth mainly on the continuity of the spirit and the universal law of cause and effect. The Buddhist theories of continuous consciousness, of rebirth and karma, are based on this concept.

## Good Deeds, Bad Deeds

*So karma can be understood as the union of action and effect. In other words: human beings become what we have done. In a certain sense, our actions even determine*

*the womb through which we are born in our reincarna-
tion. Does that mean that in the fate of a person we can
read that person's previous actions?*

At the moment of death, the consciousness is influenced
by all the intentions and motives, by all the deeds and
experiences of the dying person. The repayment for past
deeds determines the direction, the course of the next life.
What we have done to others will fall back on us in the
coming life. This is how the consciousness continues to
exist and is reborn together with the accumulated karma
in a new body.

This may occur in the form of an animal, a person,
or a divine being. As an example, let's take the shoot of
a tree. The effect, namely, the plant, is created from an
earlier cause, the seed. Good karma is created through
noble qualities such as frugality, contentment, humility,
patience, and forgiveness.

Bad karma can be weakened through repentance. The
bad deed must be repented of, with the firm intention of
not doing it again. We can be liberated from the incessant cycle of birth, suffering, death, and rebirth only when
our entire negative karma has been extinguished. In other
words, only when we have freed ourselves from all worldly
desires can we achieve Buddhahood.

But karma is very complex, and not everything that happens is related to karmic forces. The human body, for example, has resulted from thousands of years of development. This makes it difficult to draw the exact line of where the influence of karma is in effect and where natural laws come into play.

## Those Who Do Nothing Are Still Not Behaving Rightly

*Isn't there a danger that the thought of karma could lead us to a fatalistic attitude of resignination to our fate?*

Some Tibetans constantly say: "Yes, that is due to karma. Yes, this is due to karma...," and in this way try to avoid taking responsibility. This is, of course, wrong. The notion of karma especially shows us that we are responsible for our own fate and should take charge of our own lives. We believe that the intention is what primarily counts. As long as we want to do good, even if the result is bad there will be no unfavorable effects. On the other hand, when we do nothing even when someone is dependent on our help, this can lead to karmic entanglements.

There is a collective and an individual karma. The collective karma is related to a society, community, or family.

However, individuals — and this appears to be the decisive factor to me — are affected only by actions that they themselves have done. Everything that individual beings experience depend on their good or bad motives. They are the root of our actions and our experiences. Karma also has a metaphysical and an ethical aspect. Bad karma must be rendered ineffective through good deeds, through a good life.

## ✸ *Tibet's Look Inside*

*Is the current political situation in Tibet, which has caused Tibetans immeasurable suffering, somehow related to the collective karma of the Tibetan people?*

The current tragedy in Tibet is the consequence of the negative karma of the present generation. The conditions for this arose during the previous generation. And then, at the beginning of the last century, Tibet closed itself off too much from the world and neglected to have itself recognized as an independent state by the community of nations. The people were not interested in the developments taking place in the neighboring states, especially in China.

# The Task of the Religions

❀ ## On the Path of Good

*The world religions came from different cultural areas. They frequently developed without any knowledge of even the existence of other religions. This is especially true of the monotheistic religions, which have disassociated themselves from other belief systems with their claims of absolute truth and have even fought against those who believed differently. Is there, in spite of this, something mutual that connects all the religious persuasions to one another?*

Yes — love. Love can be the uniting force that overcomes all the other differences. All of the major religions of the world — Buddhism, Judaism, Christianity, Islam, Confucianism, Hinduism, Jainism, Sikhism, Taoism, Zoroastrianism — have similar concepts regarding the ideal of love. The ultimate meaning of their religious and spiritual exercises is active altruism. The great religious teachers of humanity want to turn their followers away from bad actions and bring them to the path of good through their teachings.

All religious persuasions seek answers to the fundamental questions of existence and give their believers ethical rules of conduct. All religions teach in their commandments that we should not lie, steal, or kill. These commandments show us the way.

I do not see any major differences here. According to my beliefs, the religions should teach their followers to see all people as brothers or sisters. This is the only way that they can learn to encounter each other in tolerance and mutual understanding.

## ❀ *The Best Medicine*

*Not all religious leaders share your perspective. Especially the various opinions about what serves the welfare of the people have filled libraries throughout the world.*

But if we spend too much time with the dogmatic differences that have arisen through historical and cultural conditions, we will become entangled in endless academic discussions. I personally consider it much more important to dedicate myself to my daily tasks and dedicate all my strength toward increasing the good in the world.

Perhaps we can compare the many religions with the different methods of healing physicians use. Good doctors know exactly what the best medicine is for their patients. But the mutual goal of all therapies is to heal the patient. I have also compared the world's religions to different foods that correspond to various needs and inclinations of people. Despite all the philosophical differences, the most important task of all religious persuasions is to make a contribution toward a happier humanity and a peaceful world.

## ✸ *Religion as a Means to Power*

*Why is there such a gap between the demands of religion and reality? Why have there been so many bloody religious wars? Isn't it a contradiction that many wars arise precisely out of religious conflicts, even though the main goal of religions should be to create peace? Examples are Northern Ireland and the inhumane conflicts in the former Yugoslavia, which were brought about by religious differences.*

Regrettably, religion is frequently used solely as an instrument of power in order to force one's will upon others. In such cases there are certainly not religious motives but very selfish ones at work. Unfortunately, religions have contributed, and continue to contribute, toward increasing separations and hostilities between people. Instead of helping, religion then creates even more problems. Especially today, it appears to me that to spread our own religion is not the most important goal. The dialogue among religions is more important.

❀ *A Personal Belief*

> *In my country, an increasing number of people are turning away from the churches and want to follow their own religious path. Should each of us develop our own personal belief?*

For me, religion is bound to a particular tradition. Many people think that as soon as they believe in something like a force or a power and, for example, say it is only coincidence that determines our everyday lives, that is religion. This is too extreme for me. I do not think that this can be called religion. When I once had a conversation with General Mao Zedong on this topic, he spoke out in general against every religion but admitted that he was not free of superstition. Religion and superstition are not related to each other at all. When I say religion, I mean a specific religion with its history and its traditional teachings.

## ❀ *Hope despite All the Affliction*

> *Your Holiness, is there a difference between people whose lives are influenced by prayer and meditation and those who lack a religious dimension?*

I believe that when we seriously follow the teachings of our religion day after day, our overall attitude toward life gradually begins to change. Especially in times of need and crisis, religion can give people trust and confidence, no matter how bad the circumstances may be. Religion shows that despite all the sorrowful experiences there is still an indestructible ultimate meaning. In a mysterious way, religion gives humanity the gift of a hope stronger than all obstacles, than all afflictions.

### ✳ *Very Few People Really Take Religion Seriously*

> *On the other hand, there are many people who may belong to a religious community but allow themselves to be guided by other values in their daily lives....*

Among the five billion people in the world, probably fewer than one billion are truly deeply rooted in a religion and doing religious exercises every day. These are people who, thanks to their beliefs, do not lose their equanimity even under the greatest challenges. For the others, this means that religion plays only a secondary role in important decisions or during a crisis. Their belief is not really deeply anchored. They may call themselves Christians, Buddhists, Hindus, or Muslims, but this is frequently nothing more than a name. When it really comes down to it, religion does not count anymore. This is why I think that the people who truly make their life decisions on the basis of their religion are not so numerous. This also shows the great urgency of determining how to reach the many people in whose lives religion no longer plays a significant role.

## ❀ *Assisi 1986*

> *Your Holiness, was the Prayer Meeting for World Peace in 1986 in Assisi, to which Pope John Paul II invited representatives of the world religions, a sign for you of how religions can work together?*

Yes; new relationships between religions were created especially through the Prayer Meeting in Assisi.

We came together and prayed, each according to our own belief and our understanding of religion. And we were also able to learn from each other and gain a new understanding of other religions. When Tibet was still isolated, we thought that our religion was the best. But now it appears to me that the encounter with other religions is mutually enriching. As I already mentioned, this is especially true because our shared task consists of standing up for the welfare of all of humanity.

## ❀ *Prayers for the World*

> *Some critical voices fear that encounters such as those in Assisi could lead to a mixing and relativizating of traditions, resulting in syncretism. . . .*

There have been critics not just in Assisi, but also at other prayer meetings. They asked how it was possible for the Buddhists to pray at all when they didn't even believe in a Creator God. But particularly during mutual prayer, these differences are not important. The only thing that counts is the fact that we are praying together at all and professing together our commitment to world peace. It is actually possible to pray together in harmony, even if one person worships a Higher Being, the other worships a Creator, and we venerate the Buddha.

## Do the Churches Support the Dalai Lama?

*Do the Christian churches support the Dalai Lama in his efforts on behalf of Tibet?*

At my meeting with the Archbishop of Canterbury, he told me that he would pray for the Tibetan people. The very next day, he called upon people to pray for Tibet. I have also met with Pope John Paul II a number of times. I think very highly of him. On such occasions, we speak about the importance of religious topics in the modern world and how to achieve a better understanding among the religions. The dialogue between Buddhism and Christianity has certainly deepened. Because the pope comes from

Poland, we can share our experiences with Communist regimes. There is a spontaneous understanding between us. It appears to me that John Paul II is a spiritual pope. An indication of this is that he called the man who wanted to murder him his "brother."

## Only One World Religion?

*Will there be just a single world religion in this millennium?*

Unity among the world religions does not mean that all religions should merge into one single world religion. Despite everything they have in common, I do not think much of a single "world religion." Then the variety of cultures and ways of life would also have to disappear. We should continue to hold on to our traditions. Some people feel attracted to Christianity because of the concept of a Creator God. Others in turn find Buddhism appealing because it concentrates solely on the individual's actions. Good reasons can certainly be found to support different approaches. We cannot simply let the differences disappear. We also cannot replace them with a single universal new belief.

In Assisi it was especially important for me that we decided to assume the responsibility for world peace together, as well as each of us in our own way. Religious traditions can exist side by side. They should neither fight against each other nor have to mix with each other.

## ✸ *Bodhisattvas Can Be Found Everywhere*

*Let's come back once again to the mutual characteristics of the world religions: Is there actually a correlation between the two religious founders of Buddhism and Christianity, Gautama and Jesus?*

Whether there is any historical correlation between Gautama and Jesus, as people sometimes claim, I do not know. Jesus lived in the Middle East, where Buddhism with its teachings of dharma, as well as Hinduism, had already existed for several centuries. There could also have been an exchange between the various cultures and religions through the traveling merchants. Perhaps the two religions influenced each other in this way.

For us Buddhists, on a mystical level, the great religious teachers who have brought major blessings to countless people through the centuries are the bodhisattvas, or enlightened beings. Jesus is one of them. To say this can, of course, be seen as the attempt to monopolize all of the great people for Buddhism. . . .

## ✻ *The Buddha Smiles, Jesus Suffers*

> *It is striking how differently Gautama and Jesus are depicted. The Buddha sits smiling on a lotus flower, and Jesus — as the ultimate image of suffering — has been nailed to a cross. . . .*

If I wanted to give you a less-than-serious response, I could say the difference is because Buddha was a prince who was persecuted by no one, whereas Jesus had the high priests and the Romans against him. They also lived under completely different social conditions. Although the Buddha's face may have a smiling and peaceful expression, suffering is still a basic element of his teachings. The Buddha was born into a very wealthy family, but he voluntarily gave up all comforts.

The Buddha subjected himself to the greatest renunciation during six years of his life. He retreated into solitude, meditated, and fasted. Only then was he able to achieve perfect enlightenment. This is why meditation is the most important religious practice in Buddhism. The life paths of both religious founders were influenced by simplicity, devotion, and self-sacrifice. They are shining examples of how we can voluntarily accept suffering for the welfare of other beings.

## *The Humility of Mother Teresa*

*You said that for Buddhists those who serve others in great devotion and to whom humanity owes much are bodhisattvas. Is Mother Teresa, who was awarded the Nobel Peace Prize, also one of them?*

Mother Teresa is an exemplar of how much someone can do with spiritual power. I met her in 1988 at the airport in Delhi. I was especially impressed by her humility. From the Buddhist perspective, Mother Teresa is certainly a bodhisattva. She dedicated her life exclusively to the poor, which is truly living the Christian faith. I do not know that I would be capable of doing what she did.

## *A Catholic Geshe*

*Your Holiness, the Trappist monk Thomas Merton familiarized you with Christianity. . . .*

I owe my deep appreciation of Christianity to him. I became acquainted with Thomas Merton in 1968 in

Dharamsala, shortly before his death. Even today, he embodies Christianity for me. Thomas Merton was a deeply religious man and full of humility. I had never experienced such spirituality in a Christian. For me, Thomas Merton was a Catholic *Geshe,* an especially learned monk. In the conversations with him, I discovered that many things are similar in Buddhism and Catholicism. Later I also met with Christians who radiated a similar quality. But this Trappist monk was the first who showed me what it means to be a Christian.

It is impressive how Christians of all denominations throughout the world offer practical help in many relief organizations. This is where we Buddhists can learn from Christians. In terms of meditation, I found it astonishing that body posture is not important in Christianity. In Buddhist meditation, the seated posture and breathing are key elements. Christians could certainly learn much from our meditation techniques.

# The One Human Race

### ✤ The Most Important Thing: A Good Heart

*When you travel, you meet with people from every region. From your perspective, beyond the cultural, historical, and geographic differences, is there something that all people have in common? Is there a human family?*

Yes, I frequently encounter people from various cultures, religions, and ideologies. Seen from the outside, there are major differences. Some of these can certainly be attributed to very different climatic conditions. When people live in the colder zones, they are forced to work harder to make a living. And the south with its luxuriant nature and its warmth has had an influence on people. I could list a great many differences — but we are all children of the one human race. We all bear the same longing for happiness and love within us. We all want to reduce suffering. We all know how important a good heart is.

This is a heart full of kindness, compassion, and love — from which hope and inner peace flow. So I believe that a good heart is ultimately the root and the source for genuine progress. Especially today, universal responsibility, which is based on love and kindness, has become for humanity a question of survival.

## ✣ *Ethics without Religion?*

*Does that mean that there is a global ethics?*

Religion and ethics are not the same. As has already been mentioned, some ethical principles can be found in all religions. Ethics can also exist without religion, however, so there are ethical beliefs not derived from a specific religion. It must also be possible for people with different, nonreligious worldviews to accept them. Some people think that ethics or morals are inseparably linked with religion. But then if they do not relate to a religious belief, they face a vacuum. They do not know how to orient themselves. This is a matter of finding guidelines that make sense to all people. Only then can we speak of global ethics.

In our age, thoughts about morals and ethics are certainly not intellectual games. Today it is a matter of survival. We all bear responsibility for protecting our planet from destruction. So we must join together to search for

mutual solutions. In earlier times, it was perhaps acceptable to insist upon national differences. But this is no
longer true (think of the modern economy). Even universal human rights are based upon the concept of one
humanity. We could say that this is a new ideology of
humanity that concerns all of us.

## ✸ *Our Beloved Mother*

> *Your Holiness, you once said that the love between
> mother and child is the foundation for all global ethics.
> What did you mean by this?*

According to our teachings, we all come into this world
countless times. This is why we imagine that every living being was at some point one of our parents. The
Buddhist tradition teaches us to see every living being
as "our beloved mother," to whom we should show our
gratitude. Both at the beginning and end of our lives, we
depend upon the kindness and care of other people. Why,
then, shouldn't we take care of other people during the
phase of our life in which we can look after others? This
relates equally as well to people who are not religious.
For every person, life begins with the relationship between

mother and child. Already on the first day, the child directs its entire trust toward its mother. This develops into a basic trust in life.

## ✾ *The War Begins Within*

*The image of the intimacy between mother and child shows that Buddhism is primarily concerned with the transformation of individual people. In the West, it seems that people usually expect more from social changes when it comes to dealing with problems. . . .*

Of course, social conditions are also important. But many conflicts and disorders from which the world suffers are directly related to human nature. For example, human aggression. This hostile attitude of human beings is also responsible for new wars constantly breaking out in the world. It can be found in almost every culture and is deeply rooted in human beings. Outer measures are not adequate to deal with this hostile attitude. Because of this, Buddhism primarily strives for transformation, for the transmutation of the individual. But this transformation does not mean that a "new human being" is created. Our good qualities should increasingly grow, and our bad ones diminish as a result.

❁ *Everything Depends on Everything*

> *In the twentieth century technological inventions in*
> *particular have caused interdependence, mutual depen-*
> *dence, to increase in almost every area....*

Because of the worldwide network, we are much more
dependent upon each other now. In earlier times, people
lived in more closed societies. Above all, they had to deal
with local or regional problems. Now it is more important
than ever for us to develop a universal sense of responsibility. Today the United Nations in particular shows us that
we are a community of peoples — even if it was created
in the shadow of World War II, and even if I consider the
veto rights of the five states in the Security Council to be
undemocratic. The conflicts in the former Yugoslavia have
shown that the world should begin to react more attentively to crises. And this is true even if we can participate
in people's suffering only in spirit.

We are all dependent upon one another. I call this
"wise egotism." With a positive and responsible attitude
toward ourselves, we also benefit others. When we think
in this manner, then there is no conflict at all between
our own interests and the common interest. This is the
only way that we have a chance of dealing with the great
dangers threatening the whole of humanity. Only through

mutual efforts will we succeed in dealing with looming dangers such as nuclear annihilation or the destruction of the environment.

## ✿ Crisis as an Opportunity

*If something takes place even in a remote corner of the globe, the whole world learns about it immediately. Yet rapid information from the theaters of war, natural catas- trophes, and plane crashes has also increased the fears of a menacing world. In view of the many images of horror, is there even a glimmer of hope left?*

It is certain that the global threats are dangerous. But if people were shaken up, then these events could become healing crises or opportunities. They force us to get to the root of our mistakes. Only when we know the cause and take resolute action can we succeed in preventing the threatening disaster. We constantly find ourselves in the tension between thinking in the short term and think- ing in the long term. There are often quick solutions that bring us rapid advantages. But it is better to search for lasting solutions. Some of the short-term advantages can prove to be harmful when seen as part of the bigger pic- ture. This is why I do not see immediate success as the decisive factor. In order to change something in the long run, we must learn — if necessary — to go without in the short run. When we have begun to act concretely against danger, then we can look toward the future with greater confidence.

## ✻ *We Are All Called Upon to Search for New Concepts*

*Do we need completely new concepts to solve today's problems?*

We must become aware that concepts originating from the nineteenth century are no longer adequate for today. Scientists in particular are called upon to search for new concepts. I sometimes have the impression, however, that the Western experts are often interested only in their own area of specialization. As a result, they may forget that their work is meant to serve the welfare of humanity. But I have also met scientists who do their work with an inner empathy and love.

The search for new concepts should certainly become one of the main concerns of the schools and universi- ties. The future in both rich and poor countries is largely dependent upon good education for the younger generation. It is important to have an education that gives young people the deepest possible insight into social and cultural relationships.

Many of the difficulties, such as increasing impoverishment in some areas of the world, the loss of ethical values, and growing violence, have developed because of people and must be resolved by people. These problems affect not only individual nations or a certain part of the world but the entire globe. The entire community of peoples is called upon to search together for solutions. In the past, much suffering arose because of ideologies and concepts that did not do justice to reality. As experience has taught us, we must find a comprehensive plan based on love and kindness.

## ❀ *Not Religious Luxury but a Matter of Survival*

> *In a sense, are the ethical commandments of religion, such as the dictates of the Sermon on the Mount, not just pious words but, today more than ever, suggestions about how people can survive?*

Yes. As we also find in many Buddhist texts, these are not just beautiful words, religious or moral teachings. The question of how we devote ourselves to all things in a loving attitude is not a "religious luxury" and not a religious dictate that we can believe or not believe. People often think that empathy and forgiveness are purely religious topics. Yet these things are related to all areas of life. The survival of this planet depends on whether as many people as possible develop a loving attitude to their environment. This spirit must be developed voluntarily. We cannot violently force it upon anyone. But if humanity does not succeed in developing this all-embracing perspective of love, then I do not know what kind of future we can expect.

# Dialogue with the Modern World

### ✿ A Bridge between Knowledge and Belief

*Some people say that Buddhism depends completely on the rational mind and intellectual argumentation. How does belief relate to knowledge?*

Today materialists and believers usually oppose each other. Buddhism is frequently attacked from both sides. For the one side, meditation appears to be an excuse to do nothing, to be lazy. The other side complains that Buddhism is just a science, not a religion. We Buddhists stand between knowledge and belief, which means that we build a bridge between the two extremes. This is another way we can make an important contribution in the future. As the great master of the Middle Way, Nagarjuna (second and third century), emphasized time and again, the spiritual path requires harmony between belief and mind. We could say that Buddhism is a spiritual-philosophical system.

We probably give knowledge more importance than belief. Many phenomena are accessible to the rational mind through logical evidence. There are, however, levels of perception that we ourselves cannot reach or cannot verify. Here we put our belief in the Buddha as a witness of enlightenment. We do not believe him blindly, however, but rather because we know that other parts of his teachings have proven to be reliable. The Buddha himself has called upon us not to believe something just because it is the words of the Buddha. Instead, we should be like goldsmiths who test the value of the gold throughout the various processes of refinement.

## The Middle Way

*And what about meditation?*

I truly believe that humanity can learn something from our ancient and very highly developed way of meditating. Our meditation can be compatible with every type of belief. As I would like to say to people everywhere on the earth time and again, world peace begins in a peaceful heart. This is nothing other than letting love and compassion grow in our own hearts, overcoming the inner unrest that plagues us all.

Modern technology has given many people a pleasant life, but it has also introduced new problems. Just think of the destruction of the environment, or the constantly growing cities with their noise, hectic pace, and shortage of housing. Spiritual peace is often missing there. Extremes are continually arising. Mahayana Buddhism in particular is concerned with finding the middle way and bringing the opposites into balance. When inner peace is missing, we cannot be content even with the greatest affluence. Especially in the everyday battle of life, it is important to develop inner calmness and clarity. With such an attitude, it becomes easier to solve our problems than if we let ourselves be overcome by such feelings as hatred, egotism, jealousy, or anger. In such moments, we are like blind people, allowing ourselves to be driven to thoughtless actions.

## The New Humanity Is the Same Old One

*The major world religions developed in a distant past under completely different conditions. Does humanity need a new kind of religion for the very different modern world?*

I imagine it is difficult for many people to understand the heart of religious concerns in a modern secularized world. Seen from the outside, without any inner empathy, religion may appear old-fashioned and no longer current.

Also lifestyles change over time, and we adopt different habits. As a result, the old religions appear in some respects to be outdated. So it is not surprising that some people think that religion has nothing to offer modern individuals today.

Yet, on the other hand, when it comes to the basic human issues, there is hardly any difference between us and the inhabitants of the earth who lived here thousands of years ago. Seen in this light, conventions and customs have hardly changed. Political and cultural changes take place only on the surface. From my perspective, humanity has changed only on the outside. Consequently, the old religions still have an important role. I am certain that if the Iceman, the five-thousand-year-old glacial mummy from the Alps, could speak, we would learn that he could well empathize with our current problems.

### ✸ *When Circumstances Demand It*

*Is there an inner dynamic in Tibetan Buddhism capable of adapting to new circumstances time and again?*

We have rules and forms that are obligations, and there is nothing we can change about them. This applies especially to the rules of the *sangha*, the community of monks or nuns. We believe that the Buddha established these rules. Of course, there can be exceptions when circumstances demand it. But in general, we change little in our traditions.

At the same time, the Buddhist scriptures indicate how important it is to continually compare all of our thoughts with reality. So what may appear wrong under certain conditions can once again be right under other circumstances; what was expressly prohibited at one time can in a completely different context even be recommended. So we are free to change some of the rules. It is important, however, that we discern these situations precisely. This is different for us than for the so-called fundamentalists who want to preserve the old at any price and don't want to adapt to the modern world.

## ✥ *Fundamentalism*

*Why are fundamentalist movements increasing everywhere today?*

My explanation for this is that religions are often turned into ideologies with which individuals fight their opponents and try to strengthen their own identities. If we want to restrain this phenomenon, we must strive especially for the sharing of religious experiences. The great differences often exist only in our imagination. Dialogue *within* a religious community is also very important. This is the only way we can weaken prejudices and grow closer to one another.

Buddhism is different from Catholicism because the hierarchal forms play a secondary role. Even if Tibetan Buddhists listen to my advice and my opinion, no one considers me to be infallible.

## ❀ *Those Who Insulate Themselves Also Isolate Themselves*

*Is it even possible to have a dialogue with people who have rigid, preconceived opinions?*

Having a relationship with fundamentalists is always difficult. It is similar to relationships with people who are completely devoted to one ideology. For example, it was not possible to have a proper discussion with the committed Communists of the former Soviet Union. But ultimately, the politicians there who realized that their society was behind the times made themselves heard. In any case, the majority of the population there did not support Communism. The totalitarian system finally came to an end, and this happened without violence and without open conflicts with the West. A similar thing occurs with religions. Movements that insulate themselves also isolate themselves. So all those who are willing to join in a dialogue will gain the upper hand.

It is obvious that there never will be a perfect humanity. What we can achieve is that increasingly more people are willing to be part of the conversation, and that they behave in a more tolerant and peaceful manner. This will push back destructive forces. This alone would be progress.

## ✸ *Two Philosophical Paths*

*In the West and in the East there are apparently different views on what progress means. In the West progress is conceived as a linear development. In Buddhism the world appears to move cyclically: everything repeats itself, and all beings pass through the same stages of life in a circular pattern.*

When we speak of the Western concept of linear development, then we also think of *society's* progressive dawning of consciousness. Buddhists are concerned with the maturation process of the *individual* that continues to develop through repeated new lives and therefore seems to move as in a circle. Here we are dealing with two different perspectives, different philosophical structures.

## ✿ *Money as the Measure of All Things*

> *The importance that money has assumed in the thoughts and actions of modern individuals is constantly increasing. Even in the most sacred areas, money threatens to become the measure of all things. For many people, money has almost become a substitute religion. . . .*

Whenever I come to the West I notice that hardly a day passes that we don't have to deal with money in some form or another. Just try to spend a single day in a modern city without money. Then you will personally experience how dependent people here are on money. They are constantly thinking: How much money is what I am doing right now worth? The West places too much importance upon the material world. With this attitude, the worldview of people and the value they place on things has fundamentally changed. At the same time, everyone knows that human feelings such as love and devotion to others cannot be measured with money.

All too frequently, wealth does not give us a happy and contented life. On the contrary, many rich people become slaves to their money because they are constantly worried about trying to increase their possessions. As a result they live in a continually hectic state. They do not know serenity and equanimity toward material things. When we live in such a world of restlessness, it is important to distance ourselves time and again and rediscover our inner peace.

Things are often different in the poor countries of the South. People can eat the plants they find in the natural world there, and these don't cost anything. They are extremely poor, but they also don't have to constantly think about money. When I still lived in Tibet, I was not allowed to deal with money at all. And even today, fortunately, I don't have to look after my own finances. My private office monitors all income and expenses. But even we Tibetans must earn money and cannot live just from air. In particular, we have recently been reminded of this because the government in exile has a two-million-dollar shortfall. . . .

## ❀ *Between Asceticism and Pleasure*

*How does Buddhism deal with a money-centered way of thinking?*

Here as well, we look for the middle way to avoid extremes like asceticism and hedonism. It is also important for people who are not religious to detach themselves from greed and become frugal. Those who do not know moderation will always want to have even more. Even if they owned the whole world, they would not be satisfied. Moreover, the rich are often very lonely. They can never know if others love them for themselves or for their wealth and influence. When the wealth is lost, the many false friends usually disappear like snow in the sun's heat. But this is when a person depends on a genuine friendship. In the West, I was once invited to the home of a very affluent man. He lived in an elegant and beautiful house. But there were many little bottles with sedatives and sleeping pills in the bathroom. This has become a symbol for me — that even if someone has everything it doesn't mean that person is even close to being happy.

This is true not just for Buddhists. Christian monks and nuns also strive to live a simple life in moderation. They also know that money, wealth, and fame do not ensure lasting happiness. This is why these things can never become the ultimate goal for us.

## The Rich West Is Disappointed

*Your Holiness, Tibet has long ignored the scientific findings and technological achievements of the modern world,*

> *but instead it has maintained high moral standards. In*
> *the Western world, which is oriented completely toward*
> *technology and the natural sciences, the spiritual values*
> *are deteriorating more and more. Is there a third way*
> *between these extremes?*

My main concern is finding a harmony, a balance between
the external world of the material and the inner world of
the spirit. If we want to solve the problems of humanity,
this cannot be achieved without the middle way between
economic growth and inner human maturity. I see nothing
negative about technological and material progress per se.
The poor countries of this world urgently need technological help to fight poverty. Technology can have a very
beneficial effect here.

Many of my conversation partners in modern society
complain in bitter disappointment about the excesses of
materialism. That surprises me. Otherwise, people here
seem to be so proud of progress. This only shows that
despite the progress in our age, human beings remain
searching beings. We long for a deeper meaning in our
existence. In their constant struggle for existence, modern individuals need not lose their peace of mind. Today
more than ever, it is up to religions to help people who

are completely preoccupied with the things of the outer world to find their emotional balance.

## ✸ *Behind the Beautiful Exterior Lives Fear*

*Many people do not find peace of mind. In our cutthroat society, there is a steady increase in the number of the emotionally ill, and the suicide rate is increasing. . . .*

We must strive for a balance between material progress and ethical values, between knowledge and wisdom. In the Western world, with its affluence, a great fear, a strong feeling of emptiness and pointlessness, often hides beneath the beautiful surface of the "good life," because people take the material world too seriously. Those who succumb to the illusion that they can buy the meaning of life grow unhappy. Technology, science, and progress only make the outer conditions of life easier; they do not change any of the fundamental human problems. There is still suffering, poverty, and fear.

## ✸ *There Is More Than "Either-Or"*

*In the schools, even little children are drilled to develop their intellectual abilities. Over the course of the school years, we accumulate an extensive amount of knowl-edge. But human values usually just play an incidental role....*

On my lecture tours I am constantly surprised by how the people in the West enjoy learning. The listeners have their tape recorders running or take notes. Tibetan or Chinese Buddhists, for example, are very different. They may sit very attentively but are not as enthusiastic about wanting to learn. Time and again, I am impressed by the initiative and the hunger for knowledge that I encounter here.

But I have also discovered that many people think exclusively in categories of black-and-white and either-or, overlooking in the process how much everything is dependent upon everything else and is connected to everything else. People easily forget that there are more than two points of view.

Perhaps this is because Western education is almost solely oriented toward the development of intelligence and the accumulation of as much knowledge as possible. In this process the development of the heart is probably neglected. Certainly this has historical roots. In earlier times, it was the churches that primarily attended to moral and spiritual matters. But their influence is disappearing today.

As a result, children are certainly lacking something essential in their upbringing. There must be a balance between the brain and the heart. I think that a heartless human being with a very well-functioning brain is a dangerous troublemaker. I value someone more whose intelligence is less developed but who has a good heart.

## Damage Caused by Civilization

*And what about the young Tibetans? Do they receive a balanced education?*

In the Tibet of earlier times, the monasteries were responsible for education, even in remote areas. It can sometimes be a mistake when children just seven years old take their first vows. In many cases they hardly comprehend what it means. It sometimes appears to me that the Christian system for monastic life is better. A person enters a monastery only as an adult, after a period of careful consideration during which this decision can be closely examined.

In terms of the education of Tibetans today, the youth who live abroad, in countries such as India or Switzerland, are much better off than the young people inside Tibet. But even here, I have been told, there are dishonest young people who misuse their intelligence and want to enrich themselves at the cost of others. Several months ago, there were even two cases of murder among Tibetans. It is certain that morality and ethics leave much to be desired in all countries. Our culture, too, must deal with the modern damage caused by civilization. So the Buddhists are no exception here.

I place all of my hopes in the younger generation. The responsibility for the future lies with the youth. Young people today are exposed to many bad influences through the mass media. If young people see too much violence on television, this will certainly affect their behavior. Such unpleasant pictures can cause great harm to young people. We must seriously ask ourselves what must be done so that our young people receive a balanced education. The philosopher Karl Popper, with whom I met several times, emphasized time and again how much our future depends on a balanced education for our young people.

## A World without Technology

*In the West there is the romantic dream of an ideal world without all-destructive technology. Are technological achievements and scientific progress, as you have already suggested, basically positive for you?*

Even in my childhood, I was already very interested in technological innovations and the discoveries of natural science. I am convinced that Western science with its logical thinking has made an important contribution to solving the age-old problems of humanity. Will these new findings and discoveries, however, be used for the benefit of humanity or for its destruction? Today, the nightmare of the entire globe being destroyed with one strike could become a reality. But in recent decades, Western thinking has changed considerably. Many scientists have told me in conversation that they are proceeding from a new point of view that embraces the world as a whole. In their view, thinking and feeling should no longer be poles apart.

## ❄ *Like the Fingers of One Hand*

*Even up to the eighteenth century, it was still possible for very gifted people to grasp almost the entire mass of knowledge. Since then we have become ever more specialized. Who today still has the overview?*

Our planet is being shaken by many crises today. It is not enough just to pray. All of us are called upon to put our abilities to the service of humanity. Science should not be permitted to be an end in itself. It must serve the welfare of humanity. I sometimes compare the various branches of knowledge — technology, education, and religion — with the fingers of one hand. The hand is the person; it is humanity. Individual fingers can be lost, but without the hand the fingers have no purpose. We should never forget that all the sciences, ideologies, and political systems, as different as they may be, should serve to make people happier. We should never lose sight of this goal. We should also never permit our own view of the world to become an end in itself. Humanity must always have priority.

Today I see encouraging signs that science does not have to stand in contradiction to religion and spirituality. In the past few years, I have discovered this in conversations with biologists, psychologists, quantum physicists, and cosmologists. We frequently spoke about how there is a relationship between the findings of natural science, the human mind, and the human soul. In quantum physics, it has been realized that in addition to the tiny particles that have been discovered there is also another force besides material energy.

## ❁ The Dalai Lama Is Interested in Physics

*Your Holiness, so you are also interested in the latest developments in the natural sciences.*

Yes, and I especially like to read books about biology and astronomy, but also about physics. Although I have never had the opportunity to study physics, there are Western scientists such as Carl-Friedrich von Weizsäcker whom I practically consider to be my professors. A number of times, I was able to follow their lectures for several hours. Thanks to their instruction, I can more or less find my way in this difficult area. But the impression of having understood everything disappears very quickly whenever the instruction comes to an end!

# Spiritual Crisis in a State of Affluence

## ✸ Even an Atheist Can Abide by This

*In view of the great dangers that humanity faces, many people feel insecure. How can individuals overcome the feeling of helplessness, the feeling that there is nothing they can do and that their his efforts are largely in vain?*

What every person can and should do is help others. This means that we should share and relieve the suffering of other people. "A sorrow shared is a sorrow halved." This moral principle applies to most cultures and religions. And we must not exclude anyone from this — not even our adversaries. Whether we live in the South, the North, the East, or the West, we are all members of one human race and have the same worries and needs. This ethical principle is not bound to a specific religion. Even an atheist can follow it. It is therefore not at all important whether we believe in God or the idea of rebirth. We can always do good, even today when we are afraid of the dangers that the future may bring.

## *False Gurus*

*So it's that simple? And yet there is a growing group of people who are cashing in on the lack of orientation among their fellow human beings. The number of false gurus is constantly increasing. It is becoming more and more difficult to distinguish between the genuine spiritual leaders and the charlatans.*

In response to this, I can only say over and over that a healthy dose of skepticism must be part of the search for truth. We should not blindly believe what someone says. It can become disastrous if we rely on people and do not critically examine their teachings. Even the most beautifully spoken thoughts should not delude us about the true meaning of the words. In any case, we should first be well informed about which groups we are actually dealing with.

Wishful thinking is especially dangerous in this case, when we do not want to accept reality. Only when we follow our doubts and discover the contradictions can we form an opinion and gain a clear insight. Only in comparison with other religions and philosophies can we recognize the elements of which the supposedly new teachings are composed. Then we soon will see whether what is being praised as the latest discovery is really just old hat.

Once someone has fallen for a sect, that person will hardly be capable of judging whether the supposed spiritual leader is speaking the truth. This then leads to dependence and a lack of freedom. It is naive to believe everything without forming a personal opinion. Each of us bears the responsibility for our own life and cannot relinquish it to a group. Sects disassociate themselves from others. I consider this to be very wrong. The conversation with people who think differently is very important. For this reason, and according to Tibetan tradition, I was taught by masters of different schools.

## The Game of Esotericism

*In recent decades, numerous exotic and esoteric currents have spread in the West. Some of them have even adopted the Buddhist way of thinking.*

This means that very different spiritual tendencies from other cultures and traditions are mixing with each other.

It is difficult for me to find my way through all of this. But in relation to Buddhism, I would like to say that it can even be dangerous for the unpracticed, lacking a teacher, to devote themselves to certain tantric practices out of curiosity and "playing" around. People can suffer from emotional disorders if they practice certain yogic techniques in the wrong way. There is definitely a reason why the tantric teachings of Buddhism are secret knowledge and emphatically not to be learned by just anyone taking a quick class.

## Buddhism in the Religious Supermarket

*In the West, there is a growing criticism and distaste for our own culture and religion. People go to distant places and experiment with all types of "methods of enlightenment" from foreign cultures. People are looking for more and more new things religions have to offer. That almost makes Buddhism like merchandise in the supermarket of religions and philosophies. . . .*

And how should the seekers find their way in this supermarket today? Where will it lead when people constantly change their religious path? Once individuals have decided on a path, then they should stay with it. For example, it would make little sense to intensively meditate for a few months and then completely stop — only to start again at some later time. Only when we perform the religious practices like meditation or prayer every day do they have an effect. Only then do we attain inner maturity. People in rich countries have become much too impatient. In the age of machines, everything appears to function at the push of a button — even religious enlightenment. Even if many people would like to believe this, they are wrong. We certainly do not become enlightened beings in this manner.

Let's take an example from everyday life and imagine that we go into a restaurant and order all the tempting dishes on the menu. We take a little taste of everything but do not completely finish any of the dishes. In the process, we are sure to just upset our stomach instead of being strengthened by the meal. This is quite similar to trying one meditation exercise today and a different one tomorrow, just so we can experiment with them. This is certain to cause more harm than good.

## Not Out of Enthusiasm for the Exotic

*Your Holiness, how would you respond to someone who says to you: "I have heard the Dalai Lama. What he*

*says has convinced me, and I no longer feel at home in
the Christian world. I would like to become a Buddhist."*

Individuals who give up their old religion should not do
so out of effusive enthusiasm for the exotic, nor in conflict
with their own culture. They should continue to respect
the religious communities from which they come and not
consciously separate themselves from them. Every religion
serves humanity in its own way. So I am not attempting to
convert other people to Buddhism or necessarily propagate
my religion. The only decisive factor for me is what I as
a Buddhist humanist can do for the happiness of other
people.

But it is true that in the last few decades, interest in
Buddhism has grown steadily, especially in Europe and
North America. Today, there are more than five hundred centers for Tibetan Buddhism around the world. I
am obviously very pleased about this. In order to intro-
duce Buddhism to many people, I have celebrated various
religious ceremonies in countries where people know very
little about this religion. By doing this, I also want to make
my religious contribution to world peace.

I will repeat this, however: a conversion to Buddhism
should be thoroughly considered. A spontaneous change
of religion has almost always proved to be difficult and

can lead to serious emotional disorders. Anyone who converts to Buddhism should be modest and not want to do everything differently from top to bottom with the excessive religious enthusiasm of the convert. This is what we are advised to do by an old Tibetan proverb that tells us: "Change your consciousness, but leave your exterior as it is."

# Support in Life

### ✹ Enlightenment without Drugs

*If I have understood you correctly, Buddhism is any-
thing but an escape from the world. Some people in the
West justify drug consumption by saying that people in
many ancient religious cultures took drugs for meditative
purposes.*

I think that drugs should fundamentally be rejected.
Spiritual development must be achieved through inner
maturity and not through external influences. A person
who takes drugs loses the ability to think clearly. Mental
alertness is especially important in our meditations. The
inner enlightenment that we strive for must be achieved
through mind training and daily work on inner perfection — and quite definitely not through narcotic drugs.
A person who takes drugs wants to escape the troubles
of everyday life instead of facing reality as it actually is.
This is why balancing human nature is very important in
all cultures and societies, whether this involves our own

health or how people live with one another. Basic ethics apply here whether or not a person is religious.

## ❁ *Progress and a Crisis of Meaning*

*Never before has there been so much affluence for such large segments of the population in the West. And yet more and more people appear to be asking: Does this whole thing — do our lives — have any kind of purpose?*

Yes, we see that in many parts of the world the standard of living has been raised significantly. But with the latest findings, with an increasingly higher level of knowledge, we have not succeeded up to now in making people more peaceful and happy. The number of people who can read and write has increased to a degree that was previously unknown. Despite this, we cannot say that humanity has improved itself by its behavior.

To the contrary: inner unrest and discontent seem to have increased. So-called progress does not appear to make life easier for us. It also demands its price. When inner progress, which means the sense of responsibility for ourselves and others, does not kept pace with outer progress, then we become increasingly imbalanced. It is high time for us to reflect and think about what we must change. If we do not do this, the result could be undesired consequences for future generations.

After all, we know from daily experience that when we face life with confidence in the morning, we succeed more easily. Then we can better master the challenges that each day has in store for us. We can even bear bad news with a more balanced and satisfied attitude.

However, if we are in a bad mood and are discontent, even the most beautiful things will rub us the wrong way. Then we are gripped by anger and hatred for ourselves and others. Then we no longer feel good in our own skin. We cannot enjoy a beautiful flower, the song of a bird, or the smile of a child. This shows how important it is for us to live in harmony with ourselves. Whether we assume a high position in human society or are very simple people, we all long for peace of mind and a peaceful coexistence with others.

### ❈ *Above All, Children Need Warmth*

*So you see a correlation between material progress and the Western crisis of purpose. Perhaps we could also make the following comparison: people who live in affluence can usually keep their houses warm without too much*

> *difficulty. Yet the rich West is experiencing an "Ice Age of the Emotions."*

This already begins in the parents' home. Parents must provide not only outer warmth for their child but also inner warmth. They must create an atmosphere with a sense of security in which the child feels love and acceptance. There are many unwanted children whom the parents hardly care about. The result of this can be that later, when they become teenagers, they do not want to continue to live. They are so desperate that they put an end to their lives because they were never allowed to experience in their parents' home how valuable and meaningful their life, and human life in general, is.

Loving-kindness toward a newborn child is the precondition for the child to develop properly on the spiritual and physical levels. This even applies to the period before an infant can understand the meaning of words. People may think that it isn't so important what they say to such a small being since the infant doesn't even understand the words. Yet doctors who specialize in the development of children's brains have assured me that the weeks right after birth are decisive for the development of the human brain.

Even cuddling a baby has a beneficial effect on the baby's later spiritual development. Even a child feels how important love is for a human being. We notice at the very beginning of our lives whether or not we are experiencing compassion and loving-kindness. Love is the source of our life. It is as important for human beings as water is for fish.

## ✸ *From Generation to Generation*

> *If parental love influences even the intelligence of a child, then we could say that a lack of it becomes noticeable later in professional life. So human society is dependent upon this love in many ways. . . .*

Children who grow up in the loving atmosphere of their parents' home will tend to have healthy emotional development. They will also learn better at school and be more successful. But the loving approach to children and young people should not be limited just to the parental home. It also makes a big difference how teachers approach their students, for example. If they are cold, unfriendly, and unjust to the students, the students will be less likely to enjoy learning. On the other hand, if the teachers show affection, compassion, and understanding, students will follow the instruction with much more interest. Aversion and impatience will hardly motivate them to achieve. Later, when they start their own families, they can also give their children a happy parental home. This is like a chain that stretches out from generation to generation.

Someone who must grow up without affection and is damaged as a result is in a completely different situation. Those who have not experienced love do not know what it is. This often makes their relationships with other people difficult. This could be considered the foundation for general ethics independent of religions: passing on to others the understanding, compassion, and affection that we ourselves have experienced. During the initial period of human life, love is also one of the most important preconditions for the balanced development of human nature. If it is missing, then people feel insecure throughout their lives and are plagued by all kinds of fears.

## Using Fear to Do Business

*Even the theme of fear has become a business. Fear appears to be the most frequent emotional affliction of our time. Many psychiatrists and psychotherapists have developed therapies against fear, yet the number of people tormented by fears continues to increase. What can we do?*

In modern large cities, people may live in material comfort, but they are very lonely. I am surprised at how many individuals who constantly meet other people can express their true feelings only to their pets. It is certain that the hard battle for survival in mass society results in people encountering each other with fear and mistrust.

And then there are horrible reports from the media as well. Every morning we are confronted anew with sad news on the radio, on television, and in newspapers — violence, crime, wars, and catastrophes. I cannot remember a single day where I did not hear some report of horror. Today more than ever, human life appears to be exposed to a world full of dangers. No generation before us has had to deal with so much bad news. At some point every empathetic human being will ask: What kind of world is this in which so much suffering occurs? And people become afraid of such a world.

## ❁ *Worrying Changes Very Little*

> *A hymn by Paul Gerhardt, a German poet from the seventeenth century, has these words: "Because of our worries and our grieving and our self-inflicted torment, / God takes away nothing at all. We must pray about it." Worrying usually makes everything worse. . . .*

That is a beautiful thought. For us, this means: if there are worries that we can do something about, then there is no reason to despair. But if there is nothing we can change, then despair will not help. So why should we worry if a problem can be solved? If there is a solution, then we don't have to be afraid. But when something cannot be changed, then we must yield to it. Worrying just takes away necessary strength. It is useless. I usually follow this rule: hope for the best and be prepared for the worst.

After all, in Buddhism we believe in karma, in the "law of cause and effect." When we experience great suffering, it can be helpful when we know that it has been caused by our own previous mistakes. Then we are no longer helpless but take responsibility for our own fate. Such an attitude can be helpful. It can allow the fear and despair to disappear.

People are allowed to hope for many things. When a hope is not fulfilled, this is not a catastrophe. Life with its many possibilities goes on, and other wishes are fulfilled. If we put all our eggs in one basket, then a failure may cause us to fall into deep despair and depression, or we may even take our life out of disappointment. But with the right attitude, no one needs to be this hopeless.

### ✸ *For Us, Death Is a Close Companion*

*Your Holiness, are there moments in which even you are
seized by anxious unrest, such as when someone flying
fears a disaster with no chance for survival?*

As a child, I was afraid of the dark, which I obviously no
longer am. My primary concern is not about myself and my
personal security. I think of the six million Tibetans who
put their trust and their hope in me. When we can control
our spiritual powers, we do not have to be afraid, even
when an airplane crashes. I prepare myself for death every
day. For us Buddhists, death is something very natural, a
phenomenon that is part of the cycle of existence, samsara.
Death is not an ending. It is something very familiar for
us; we almost instinctively accept it, and we do not need
to fear it. I imagine dying to be something like exchanging
worn-out clothes for new ones. This could be something
wonderful.

### ✸ *Age, Illness, and Death: The Messengers of the Gods*

*Since time immemorial, humanity has been concerned
with the question of suffering — even if many people in
our affluent society do not like to be reminded of this. In*

*Buddhism, age, illness, and death are called the "Messengers of the Gods" (deva-duta). They are intended to make people conscious that our existence is sorrowful and impermanent.*

We are meant to be brought to the path of liberation in this way. Daily meditation is very helpful in doing this. Instead of running away from the thoughts of aging, illness, and death, letting ourselves be distracted by a hectic pace and noise, we sit down and become familiar and intimate with these realities. When we repeatedly become aware that our life is closely connected with suffering, dying, and death, the awareness will become our second nature. Then we can accept life in happiness and in suffering as a unity. We do not need to fear the thought that all of us must eventually say goodbye to everything.

Suffering can also be a school of life. When we look at the biographies of influential people, we see that in many cases they become much stronger precisely because of difficult experiences. Someone who is pampered and has everything can fall into deep despair when even the smallest difficulties arise.

When I compare the generation that experienced World War II with the youth of today, I feel that this view is confirmed. It is certain that there is nothing that is only bad. Sometimes we must change our perspective and then we see in retrospect that even the saddest occurrence can also conceal a valuable experience within it.

## ❁ *Light and Shadow*

*It is also important that we learn to keep a certain distance from ourselves so that we do not get stuck in sad occurrences or snap because of them. . . .*

Meditation helps us with this. We can, for example, imagine how harmful it is to constantly be unhappy and discontented. When we think about the value and purpose of life, then two perspectives open up to us: on the one hand, we gain trust and security; on the other hand, we recognize our limitations and are reminded that we are mortal. Even those who do not believe in life after death must also deal with the fact of aging. The desire to have a long life and yet never grow old — the desire for eternal youth — remains an unrealizable dream. Age is a part of all life. No power, no science, no modern technology can stop this natural process. So it is much better to accept this basic fact and make friends with it than to struggle against it or suppress it.

If we refuse to see the shadow aspects of human life, we won't be prepared for such blows of fate as the loss of someone close to us or a serious illness. Those who are completely unprepared will be overcome by misfortune. In Buddhism we believe, as I have mentioned, that suffering is a consequence of our evil thoughts, our feelings of hatred, our bad deeds, our ignorance. This is what we call negative karma. In a coming rebirth, we could return as an animal and not as a human being. In a human existence, however, we can deal with suffering in an appropriate way and reduce negative karma better than animals can.

## Experiences While Dying

*How during meditation does a Buddhist prepare for death?*

During my own meditation, I think about my own death eight times a day. As I do this, I let the individual phases of the death process occur before my inner eye. It is important to repeat this exercise constantly. But even this incessant preparation for death obviously does not give me any ultimate security. I do not know in advance whether I will truly stand the test in my last hours when the time comes.

Television viewers who were horrified by the gruesome pictures from the war in Bosnia, for example, are still dealing with the fear of their own mortality. We can assume one of two attitudes toward death: ignore it or very consciously accept the fact that at some point our life will come to an end. Since it is obvious that we must die, it is pointless to worry about it. When we learn to think in this manner, the fear of death can be diminished. Of course, this does not mean that death will be conquered as a result.

We Buddhists believe that the deepest and most healing experiences can occur when we are dying. The way in which we die has an influence on the circumstances of our rebirth. We should leave this life in peace and free ourselves from bad deeds. This is why many great masters leave their lives during meditation and practice dying. In tantra, there are important exercises that are done during sleep or in dreams, and these are intended to prepare the person for death.

## Everyone Dies Differently

*Probably no one in German literature has written as profoundly about death as the poet Rainer Maria Rilke. "O Lord, give each of us a death of our own. The dying that comes from a life that had love, meaning, and suffering in it," he wrote in his* Book of Hours.

There are many ways to die. It is certain that when individuals die a natural death, they are better prepared for it and can consciously leave this life. Then they will not lose their inner peace. This spiritual attitude influences the new reincarnation. According to the Buddhist perspective, death can occur because the life force or the "karma earned," the good deeds, have been exhausted. Other people suffer a violent death.

A nurse once told me that very religious people often die full of fear because they are afraid of "the Last Judgment." After a fulfilled life, individuals can calmly die with the feeling of having done their best. People who have done good deeds in their lives usually leave this life in a peaceful way. Then the fear of death disappears. It is different for those who have been entangled in many harmful deeds. People who have mostly done bad deeds and harmed others often have feelings of guilt in their last hours.

✵ *Greed Is the Root of Many Evils*

*We also tend to say that no one can escape the curse of evil deeds. So why is it so difficult to do good and avoid evil?*

We must search for the causes of evil deep within ourselves. As soon as we let ourselves be dominated by the reprehensible powers of evil, we accumulate bad karma and harm ourselves the most. For this reason alone, we must always make an effort to strengthen the good within us.

According to the Buddhist teachings about the soul, most of our difficulties come from our passionate desire to own the things that we mistakenly think are imperishable. In particular, greed, the desire to own something, makes us aggressive. This attitude then determines our actions. Ultimately this is also the root of all warlike actions. This has certainly been the case since the dawn of humanity, but under current modern conditions this attitude has become even more threatening. We must not let ourselves be poisoned by blindness, greed, envy, and aggression. Almost all of the crises in this world occur because of these "poisons."

I grew up in the tradition of Mahayana Buddhism and believe that love and compassion are the best guarantee for mastering, above all, our continual interior challenges. The main theme of the meditation practice I do every day is all-encompassing compassion and mercy and the interdependence of all forms of existence.

This also helps me in my attitude toward the Chinese. If I allowed myself to feel hatred, anger, and rage toward the Chinese, this would not be a sign of strength. As a result, I would lose my inner peace. Someone might object that spiritual exercises aimed at changing the human heart contribute little to solving political challenges. But many of the fundamental problems in politics are, above all, created by people's negative attitude. In the long run, these problems can be solved only when human beings change.

## Bad Thoughts Are Our True Enemies

*According to the Buddhist view, where does the evil in the world come from?*

In Buddhism we have various explanations for the bad qualities in people. First, there is the belief that many bad things of today are effects from previous lives. Then we also consider the bad influence of other people. If we find ourselves in bad company with envious and hard-hearted people, this can rub off on us. We are certain to experience negative things from such people and can lose our basic trust in humanity. There is also the danger that we are concerned only with our own advantage instead of thinking of the well-being of others.

Our true enemies are our own bad thoughts. We may be able to run away from external enemies. But hatred and anger remain with us, even when we lock the doors behind us. When we have negative thoughts, we harm ourselves the most because even the most beautiful things no longer make us happy. I remember how I once attempted to repair a clock. Although clock repair is one of my favorite activities, when I repeatedly failed to fix it, I struck the clock and broke everything.

## The Beam in Our Own Eye

*But usually we think the other way around. We don't want to see our own mistakes but can talk endlessly about the bad qualities of others. This is also what Jesus meant with the metaphor: "How can you say to your brother, 'Allow me to take the splinter out of your eye' while the beam is in your own eye?" This is how the "brother" quickly becomes the enemy.*

Yes, the only evil that should truly affect me is the evil in my own heart. External hostilities can pass, but the inner enemies such as anger, hatred, and desire will remain. The same thing applies to every human being: I am my own worst enemy with my dependence, my desire, and my hatred. The enemy in our own hearts will always remain an enemy. We should not make any compromises with our evil tendencies. Bad thoughts cannot achieve anything good. They must be brought under control because otherwise we will not attain inner peace. Seen in this way, our true enemy, the restless troublemaker, lives within us.

On the other hand, the *external* enemy of today can sometimes become the best friend of tomorrow. In my own life, I have frequently learned the most from those whom I considered to be my enemies.

## ✵ Enemies Become Friends

*Learn from our enemies?*

We should practice healing kindness and tolerance not only toward our family and friends but especially toward our adversaries. Seen in this way, my enemy is my true friend. My enemy is the touchstone for my inner strength, my tolerance, and my respect for others, especially strangers. Mahayana Buddhism places great emphasis on this point.

## ✸ We Are All Human Beings

*Tolerance and understanding for strangers are becoming increasingly important now that cultures are getting closer to each other and mingling. Yet despite this, a xenophobic attitude is spreading through almost all of Europe. Violence against foreigners has increased in Germany. . . .*

But I take it as a good sign that the public has expressed such shock about this violence. As long as the people reject foreigners, politicians can do very little about it. The important thing is for us to encounter strangers with a friendly attitude. As we do this, we should always keep in mind that strangers feel just like we do. This is the only way for the barriers we inwardly erect between ourselves, our family, and strangers to fall. This is the only way that genuine contact with our fellow human beings is created.

Among other things, the feelings of hatred toward foreigners are an expression of fear of the unknown. When strangers meet each other, they are initially cautious and reserved. But such fears can be reduced. When I meet people I do not yet know, I pay little attention to their position or whether they are rich or poor. What counts for me is their facial expression, their smile, and the look in their eyes. This tells me more about individuals than anything written on their passports. Every time I speak with someone from a different culture, I may feel that certain things make us different from one another — and yet we are all human beings.

When children from Africa, Europe, or Asia meet, they don't have any difficulty coming together and playing together. After all, children don't pay attention to cultural differences. If they get along well with each other, they become friends without paying attention to race or skin color. This shows that there is the one large community of peoples.

# Different Ideas About Happiness

## ✸ Happiness and Unhappiness

*Your Holiness, you frequently emphasize that all people strive for happiness. But don't we all differ greatly in our concepts of happiness?*

Happiness has many levels. I imagine happiness as a harmonious interplay of inner peace in the hearts of individual people and as external world peace among societies. And I wish for the greatest possible affluence for all the inhabitants of the earth. Poverty and misery do not create a happy life. We must be able to satisfy our basic needs. We need food to eat, clean water, and a roof over our heads. This applies to every culture.

Some people think that those who enjoy life in the lap of luxury and take pleasure in their days without any major efforts lead a truly happy life. But wealth is no guarantee of happiness. Often the worries increase when the money increases. The more we own, the more we can lose. We have barely acquired something and already we are afraid of losing it. Those who buy something out of pure greed will soon notice that there are others who possess even more. This path will never lead us to inner peace. There are two ways of experiencing happiness and suffering: on the spiritual or on the physical level. I believe that the spiritual level is the decisive one. So it is very important for us to exercise our mind. This is how we can encounter misfortune with greater serenity and become more receptive to happiness.

## ❀ Human Kindness at the Department Store?

*The consumer society is based on the idea that buying makes us happy. People are constantly being persuaded that they still need this or that for ultimate happiness. Even our religious holidays have degenerated into celebrations of consumption.*

That buying makes us happy is an illusion. Although science and technology have made an important contribution to people's well-being, they will never be able to produce happiness for them. I have seen many opulent department stores in the United States and Europe where every possible type of merchandise is offered, but I have never seen one where human kindness is for sale. Material progress has given people a type of happiness that depends only on external conditions. But true happiness comes from the hearts of the people and is not bound to any type of goods. Kindness and happiness must grow within our own hearts. Although it is now possible to transplant hearts, there is no operation that can give us a loving and kind heart.

When we are willing to lead a modest life, then we are also content. A simple lifestyle is very important for being happy. When we are happy with what we have, when we're satisfied and do not constantly want something new, we will experience contentment and the joy of existence. It is also possible to be happy in simple clothing, or even in rags, and live in an unassuming apartment. And we can be filled with deep joy when we succeed in detaching ourselves from false inner attitudes and ties.

## ❀ The Highest Goals

*Does the search for happiness determine the purpose of our life?*

Contentment, joy, and happiness are certainly the highest goals in life. And the source of happiness is an empathetic and loving heart. Even from the very first moment that human beings enter this world, they long for happiness and instinctively try to avoid suffering. It doesn't matter at all which class of society individuals are born into, what education they have, which ideology they grew up with, or which country they live in. Even if I don't know of any political system that is superior to all the others, all people have a right to happiness in their own country.

# Peace and the Environment

### ✤ In the Spirit of Mahatma Gandhi

*You are certainly also thinking of your homeland, Tibet, when you speak of happiness in one's own country. In an epoch of increasing violence, the Dalai Lama embodies nonviolent resistance like very few others. You have committed yourself in an unshakeable way to nonviolence. All of your suggested solutions for peace are based on tolerance and mutual respect in the spirit of Mahatma Gandhi and Martin Luther King, Jr.*

I feel especially indebted to the teachings of Mahatma Gandhi. As I said in my speech on the occasion of my Nobel Prize in Oslo in 1989, I saw the prize as a sign that we Tibetans have not been forgotten. Even though we have fought with peaceful means, we have drawn attention to our plight. This was also a recognition of the values that are important to us — such as respect for all forms of life and belief in the power of the truth. I believe that dialogue is the only way to find a lasting solution for the issue of Tibet.

Some things may be achieved in the short run through violence, but in the long run, violence makes everything more difficult. For this reason, I am committed to nonviolent resistance and actions without violence.

## ✤ *Resistance without Weapons*

*When we think of the repeated uprisings in Tibet, it could look like the politics of nonviolent resistance have begun to crumble there.*

No, I don't think so. In 1987, I described in a five-point peace plan how the Tibetan issue could be resolved: Tibet should form an independently governed, democratic entity, but China would continue to be responsible for its foreign policy. Since the Chinese side did not react at all, I withdrew this suggestion in 1991. The far-reaching concessions to the Chinese ruling powers have brought me a great deal of criticism from Tibetans. Be that as it may, I still continue to support nonviolence.

## ✤ *Even the Chinese Are Grateful*

*Are there circumstances in which the use of violence can be justified by religion?*

Yes, under certain circumstances. It all depends on the motivations and the goals that people intend to achieve as a result. If there are no alternatives whatsoever, then violence is permitted. In view of the Tibetan issue, however, an armed battle would be absolute suicide. China could wipe out the entire Tibetan people.

My conviction that nonviolence is the proper course has recently been confirmed anew. Many Chinese in China and in exile have let me know that they are grateful to me for not withdrawing from this position. In this way, we have also avoided any feelings of hatred toward the Chinese. This was again a confirmation that my path is the right one. I am very happy about this.

## The Future of Humanity

*Seen from this perspective, does this mean that nonviolence is more than just the simple absence of violence?*

For us, nonviolence is an attitude of the mind that is coupled with love and compassion. After all, it is possible for people to speak friendly words to others with their mouths while bearing evil thoughts in their hearts. On the other hand, people can appear to be hardened but

still be influenced by compassion. It always depends upon
the motivations.

Some think that nonviolence is just something for very
pious individuals. But I believe that it concerns all people
and that the future of humanity depends upon the peaceful
coexistence of all beings. We would all be endangered if
hatred and violence gained the upper hand. Especially in
view of the terrifying potential of weapons, our idea of
nonviolence has become an issue of survival. The only
way for all of us to survive on this planet is to practice
the attitude of nonviolence. Particularly in the twentieth
century, we have had to experience time and again how
much suffering and misery is caused by wars. We have
learned how much we must fear the use of weapons.

## ❀ Soldiers Do Not Accomplish Anything

*Is it possible to have a world without violence? Or is it
just an illusion?*

Unfortunately, anger, hatred, and violence are constant
contributing factors to the current conflicts whether in the
Middle East, Southeast Asia, the former Yugoslavia, or in
the clashes between the North and the South. Many trouble spots develop because one group does not understand

the differences in other people. Neither more weapons and soldiers, nor the greatest development aid can change anything about this. It must become increasingly clear to us that we human beings all have a common fate. Hatred and war do not even bring happiness to the victors. Violence always produces misery and does not bring a blessing to those who have proved to be stronger.

The Cold War has come to an end, and yet the nuclear weapons arsenals that could destroy everything still exist. Wars occur because people are driven by restlessness and destructive frenzy. Everyone always loses the war. Perhaps political leaders should hold "détente meetings" in which they could get to know each other better as people in a more casual atmosphere. They would probably develop a better understanding of one another as a result. Race, culture, and ideology must not separate us, because there is only a single humanity. This applies to war or peace, as well as to the rescue or destruction of the environment.

## A Warning from "Mother Earth" to Her Children

> For Buddhists, in contrast to Christians, human beings are not the pinnacle of Creation. They have not been called upon to subjugate the earth. . . .

Whatever concept we may have, today harsh reality forces us to rethink the situation. We Buddhists think that the planet Earth is like a "mother" to us. She is a mother who has created us human beings and provided us with all of our necessities. We are given loving care by nature. So we must also ensure the preservation of nature. In view of the devastating environmental destruction of our age, it appears that Mother Earth is saying to us today: "My children, you must be sensible. If you continue to exploit your planet like this, the only possible result is catastrophe."

Up to now, our "mother" has tolerated the bad behavior of her children. But because we are going to ever greater extremes, limitations are being set for us. There are many warning signs we should not overlook. We cannot continue to think only of our own advantages in an inconsiderate and selfish way. This planet is our home. We wouldn't dream of setting fire to our own house to warm ourselves with the flames. Where could we move when our planet is destroyed? Maybe to the moon?

## ❀ The Fish Are Swimming Again

*Today many people have begun to take the warnings of Mother Earth seriously. But it's another issue whether the initiatives taken up to now have been adequate.*

Yes, there is a "friendly ecology" that attempts to stop the destruction of the ozone layer with environmentally friendly aerosol cans. When I was in Stockholm many years ago, I saw Lake Mälar, which runs through the city. It looked like it was dead. It was so polluted that people told me there were hardly any fish living in it. When I recently returned, I discovered that the king has personally released fish into it again. The factories on the river that feeds the lake have taken appropriate measures. Efforts have been made to limit the pollution. Only if we live in a modest and sensible manner and do not waste the earth's natural resources are we living in harmony with nature. If we do not stop the destructive exploitation, the natural equilibrium will be disturbed, the number of natural catastrophes will increase, and not only humanity but also the animal and plant world will suffer as a result.

## ❀ Ahimsa

*Your Holiness, is it true that you would like to make Tibet into a peace zone?*

Yes, I would like it to be an "ahimsa zone." Ahimsa is a Buddhist word for the "noninjuring" of living beings. My dream is for the entire elevated plain of Tibet to become a place of refuge where human beings and nature could live in harmonious balance. People from all over the world could live there in peace. Tibet could become a center of peace and contribute to its spreading throughout the entire Earth.

I would like to make Tibet the largest nature preserve in the world. All the organizations dedicated to the promotion of peace and the protection of life would be welcomed there. Because of its geographic elevation, its history, and its spiritual heritage, Tibet is especially suited for playing its historical role as a buffer in the middle of a strategic zone between the major powers of Asia. So this is also the Middle Way, which remains a central concern for us Buddhists. We constantly attempt to find a balanced position between the extremes, whether as individuals, a people, or a culture.

❀ *Stark Poverty and the Good Life*

> *We are all threatened by environmental catastrophes, and yet the majority of the world's population lives in extreme poverty. . . .*

A contradiction exists in this sense. The poor countries need faster economic growth for survival, yet an increase in their standard of living destroys the environment. Without economic development, the survival of large segments of humanity is endangered. We find ourselves in a dilemma because humanity cannot go back to the standards of nineteenth-century technology. Should we close all factories and go back to being self-sufficient? Clearly something like this is not possible.

Already during the 1960s I had long discussions with an Indian who proposed that individuals should own a small piece of land and provide for their own subsistence; all of the large farms would be abolished. He was a true ecologist, even though he did not know this because the term had not yet reached India.

In considering all these questions, it is not just about us but also about future generations. The population is increasing and natural resources are getting scarcer and scarcer. For example, think of the trees: even today, we do not know the effects that the dying of forests will have on the climate, soil, and the worldwide ecology. These problems will overwhelm us if people do not stop focusing only on their own good. If our current generation does not succeed in thinking globally, then we will leave behind unsolvable problems for our children and children's children.

# Religious Freedom in Tibet

🏵 ## They Are Only Mimicking Like Parrots Now

*Your Holiness, how extensive is religious freedom in Tibet
under Chinese occupation? Can the monks practice their
religion without interference?*

The Chinese had hoped that the foundations of the
Buddhist teachings would disappear within one or two
generations. They actually believed that they would be
able to eradicate every conviction and every belief except
Marxism. For this reason, they are still trying to prevent the propagation of Buddhism through every possible
restriction. But the situation is different from region to
region. In the so-called "Autonomous Province of Tibet,"
the restrictions are more severe than in Amdo and Kham
and some of the more remote areas that are difficult for
the Chinese officials to control.

It appears that the Chinese barely understand the
nature of Buddhism. They do permit certain religious
practices such as prostrations — when people touch the

forehead, throat, and chest with folded hands and then throw themselves down in full length on the ground before getting up and repeating the motion. They are not opposed to our prayer practices such as the use of prayer wheels, lighting butter lamps, wearing prayer beads, or saying the mantra *om mani padme hum* (Om! The jewel is in the lotus, hum). But from the Buddhist perspective, these are just lesser religious exercises. The essential practice for us is the transformation of the mind, the fundamental transformation of the human attitude toward our surroundings and especially toward our fellow human beings.

In order to truly understand Buddhism, it is necessary to study it extensively. Unfortunately, there are hardly any Buddhist scholars left in Tibet today, and the few that have remained have been intimidated. They are afraid of the severe punishments looming for those who spread our teachings. Therefore I find it deplorable that religious instruction is completely inadequate in Tibet. If these circumstances continue, Buddhism there could degenerate into a religion of blind beliefs. Buddhist education takes up to eighteen years. Those who do not thoroughly study the teachings are only repeating the words like parrots, without any true understanding of the meaning. The greatest problem is finding a good teacher. There are already more trained Tibetan monks living in exile than in Tibet itself.

As a result, the monasteries there often ask me to send them well-trained teachers. The few who are still there today are already between seventy and eighty years old.

## ❈ *A Suffering People*

*How do you assess the situation in Tibet today? The Chinese say that they have released more than a thousand Tibetans from the prisons since 1987 and that no one has been executed.*

That is hard to believe. Documents show there have been at least three or four public executions during this period, that many people have disappeared without a trace, and that thousands have been abused in the prisons. They are using gruesome methods of torture such as drawing so much blood from prisoners that they die. Thanks to the commitment of many friends of Tibet, we are quite well informed about the unimaginably cruel violations of human rights.

The existence of the Tibetan people is endangered by an intentional resettlement policy moving Han Chinese to Tibet. Even now, Tibetans are already a minority in their own country. Ruthless laws do not stop at forced sterilizations or forced abortions — forced even up to the ninth month of pregnancy. During recent decades, one million

Tibetans have lost their lives. More than six hundred monasteries have been systematically destroyed. Hundreds of monks and nuns have been driven from their spiritual centers. The animal and plant world has been severely damaged, and the environment is threatened by nuclear waste dumps.

## ❀ *Soon They Will Also Think Like the Han Chinese*

*So the human rights situation in Tibet is critical?*

The situation is extremely alarming, especially because so many Han Chinese are being relocated to Tibet. As a result, more and more Tibetans are losing their jobs, living in poverty, and having — against their will — to be supported by the state. This obviously leads to major tensions. The Chinese leadership interprets even the smallest expression of vexation as political resistance. People are then imprisoned and abused, which almost always results in serious violations of human rights.

In towns where a great many Chinese live, the Tibetans are forced to speak Chinese. In time, they will also change their behavior patterns and way of thinking. Because of the strong influence of the Chinese, Tibetan culture is in jeopardy. I see my most urgent task as protecting the Tibetans from this "Chinese future."

## ✤ *The Connection to Beijing*

*Are there direct contacts between the Dalai Lama and the government in Beijing?*

Yes, there have been. There were direct contacts between the Tibetan government in exile and the Chinese in the year 1979. At that time, Deng Xiaoping had the Chinese government inform me that we could discuss anything except complete independence. Moreover, the Chinese also lived under different political systems in Hong Kong and Taiwan. For these reasons for four years I attempted to find a solution to the Tibet issue. I never spoke about complete independence but considered the idea of one country with two systems as the basis of my suggestions.

At that time, we could send three delegations to Tibet to study the situation there. Afterward we were able to speak with the Chinese leaders in Beijing about the Tibetan issue and its solution. We quickly comprehended, however, that the issue of Tibet does not exist at all for the Chinese side. They told us that there is only one problem, and that is that the Dalai Lama lived outside of Tibet. According to them, the people were doing well inside Tibet and the Tibetans were very happy under the Chinese leadership.

We, of course, pointed out that the opposite was true and let the Chinese know that a solution to the Tibet problem would not only be in the interest of the Tibetan people but would also benefit the Chinese. For this reason, it is important to look at the facts of what is actually happening in Tibet. In 1987, I described how the Tibetan issue could be solved according to a five-point peace plan. In 1988, I suggested before the European Parliament in Strasbourg that Tibet should become an independently governed democratic entity, but China should continue to remain responsible for foreign policy. These extensive concessions to Chinese rulers brought me a great deal of criticism from the Tibetans. Yet even to this day there has been absolutely no reaction from the Chinese side. Because of the silence on the part of the Chinese, I have now withdrawn my offer. Still, I am determined to continue my efforts.

## ✵ Sanctions

*How should other governments behave toward China to help the cause of Tibet? For example, do you consider sanctions to be a suitable means?*

As the most populated country on earth, China should not be excluded from world politics. Instead, it should be integrated much more into the current of international politics. But at the same time, other countries should clearly express to our Chinese friends that they are behaving wrongly. They should especially be condemned because of human rights violations. This is why I was against holding the Olympic Games in Beijing. It appears to me that the policies toward the former Soviet Union were very wise in this respect. On the one hand, a very clear and uncompromising adherence to human rights was demanded, but at the same time there were constant negotiations with the Soviets in order to improve the relationship. But when words accomplish very little, economic sanctions should be considered as a means of exerting pressure.

## ❀ When the Issue Is Justice

*Are there similarities between Marxism and Buddhism?*

I definitely feel connected to the socialist ideas of justice and brotherhood in the world through the Buddhist teachings, because the capitalistic system has its shadow aspects.

Above all, I dislike the continually widening gap between the poor and the rich.

## ✸ *A Puja for the Victims of Tienanmen*

*Are there Chinese who are interested in Buddhism?*

Tibetan Buddhism appears to be meeting with increasing interest on the part of the young Chinese, especially the intellectuals. Since ideological confusion is currently rampant not only in China but also throughout Asia, our religion could give many people support. Although Marxism remains the only officially sanctioned ideology in China, hardly anyone believes in it anymore. When money becomes the highest value, then there is the danger of apathy and cynicism toward the values of life. Especially in such a situation, Buddhism could help people find peace of mind. In 1989, I advocated the celebration of a *puja*, a memorial ceremony, for the victims of the massacre at Tienanmen Square. As a result, the interest in the cause of Tibet has grown among the Chinese. Since then we have also had contact with various movements for democracy in China.

## ✤ *Panchen Lama*

*Didn't you also recently seek a conversation with the Chinese because of the search for the incarnation of the Panchen Lama, who died in 1989?*

The government in exile approached the Chinese ambassador in Delhi with the request for help in searching for the incarnation of the Panchen Lama, the second-highest religious dignitary of the Tibetans. I consider it to be a special moral responsibility to be involved in finding this incarnation because the former Panchen Lama was deeply committed to finding the previous Dalai Lama. My suggestion to the Chinese ambassador was for qualified Tibetan monks to go to Tibet to search for the incarnation there. A negative response from the Chinese side came after three months. They let it be known that as long as the Dalai Lama lives outside of Tibet, he will not be allowed to get involved in internal Chinese matters. (Most recently, an accord seems to be in the offing in this matter — Author's note.)

## ✤ *The Government in Exile*

*Is there an exile government outside of Tibet dedicated to the interests of the country?*

Yes, in Dharamsala, India, where I live today. We do not yet have actual political parties, but there are efforts to establish them. The exile government consists of delegates elected from the exile community.

# Politics and Religion

### ❁ Politicians Especially Need Religion

*Your Holiness, you say that religion has an important role in achieving and maintaining peace in the world. What role can religion play in a world that stands completely under the dictates of political power?*

I consider it very important for religion to have an influence on politicians. Politicians need religion much more than pious people who have withdrawn from the world need it. There is a constant increase in the scandals in politics and business that can be traced back to the lack of self-discipline on the part of the responsible parties. In India, the minister-president of West Bengal once said to me with what he considered a humble attitude that he was a politician and not a religious person. I responded to him: politicians need religion more than anyone else.

When hermits in solitude are bad persons, the result is that they harm themselves alone and no one else. But when such influential people as politicians are full of bad intentions, they can bring misfortune to many. This is why religion, as continuous work on our inner maturity, is important for political rulers.

A politician must have moral principles. I am convinced of this. Seen in this light, politics and religion belong together. In the United States, church and state may be separate, but when the president takes office, he makes a vow in the name of God with his hand on the Bible. This means that God should be the witness that the president will conscientiously fulfill his official duties.

## ✸ *Noble Concepts for Humanity*

> *Throughout the world, there is an increase in scandals involving corrupt politicians. Isn't the business of politics so dirty that a pious person is better off staying away from it?*

I know that for some people, the word "politics" has come to be synonymous with immorality. They think it is better to avoid politics. Politics without ethical rules harms every society, and a life without morals is the downfall of every human being. But politics is not "dirty" intrinsically, even though many politicians have abused the high ideals and noble concepts that are meant to serve the welfare of humanity.

Many believers think that religion and politics have little relationship to each other. They consider the intervention of theologians or religious leaders in politics to be inappropriate. But this is a biased perspective. Today more than ever, ethics must play a major role in politics. As we know, it can become very dangerous when politicians disregard moral principles. At the same time, it is not so important whether we believe in God or karma. Ethics is the foundation of every religion. It is important for religious people not to retreat from the world and the society in which they live. We cannot help others by withdrawing from the world, and service to others is the basis of every religion. An extermination of the Tibetans by Chinese Communism would not only mean the end of a people, but also the end of a very highly developed culture. The entire world bears responsibility for the preservation of our ancient Tibetan culture.

# Analysis

❀ When the Iron Bird Flies

Since the 1970s, hundreds of thousands, even millions of Europeans and Americans have discovered Tibetan Buddhism and its holistic way of life. Some may be fascinated by its logical analyses, others by its splendid rituals or strict meditation. In this ancient religion, all of this merges into a synthesis that strives to show a Middle Way for all areas of life. The world took notice in 1950 when the Chinese marched into Tibet, which had been independent since 1911, and in 1959 When the Dalai Lama and many high lamas fled. As a consequence, various Tibetan centers were established in the West. Because of the noteworthy travels of the Dalai Lama to Europe and the United States, the interest in Tibetan Buddhism and its various schools has continually grown.

Many people believe that these developments have fulfilled the prophetic words of the eighth-century Indian scholar Padmasambhava, who brought Buddhism to Tibet: "When the iron bird flies and the horses roll on wheels, the Tibetan people will be scattered throughout the world like ants, and the dharma [the Buddhist teachings] will come to the Land of the Red Man."

## ❀ Alert, Serene, and Creative

Buddhism has something to say to all of us, especially because it is based upon experience. It involves the life of all sentient beings in the here and now, as well as their mutual relationship to everything that exists — or the increasingly greater interdependence of all things, as we would say today. Whoever wants to understand fundamental Buddhist ideology does not need to have any complicated theoretical knowledge at the beginning. The starting point is the insight, accessible to every thinking and searching human being, that our life and all phenomena are relative and impermanent.

Because human beings do not want to surrender to this law of impermanence and want to hold on to everything on earth, they experience life as ever more sorrowful. Every attachment to what exists, all clinging to things, becomes a cherished delusion that creates all suffering. Consequently, Buddhists believe that everything we think is important, that we absolutely want to achieve — including our worrying, our fears, and our hopes, and even our own selves — is basically just an illusion.

We are just visitors here on earth, says the Dalai Lama. We have our experiences and then we leave. But because we have come into this particular existence, we should make the best of it. This is the path that the Buddha wants to show us. We should strive for a balance between inner serenity and actively creating our world. Our restless mind, which is constantly stirred up by thoughts and feelings, should become calm. Buddhists strive for a balance that reminds us of a famous Christian prayer: "God grant me the serenity to accept the things I cannot change; courage to change the things I can; and wisdom to know the difference."

## ✸ Buddhism Has Many Faces

The scope of this book obviously does not cover an in-depth analysis of Buddhism. But it does include a brief outline of this world that may appear strange and complex to many, a sketch from the author's perspective. "Very few people may completely understand the teachings of the Buddha. But it does help when they understand a little of it," says the Buddhism researcher Heinz Bechert. During twenty-five centuries, Buddhism has spread throughout and become established in thirty Asian countries with great cultural differences.

Today there are Buddhist terms in more than twenty languages. This is the source of many linguistic and conceptual difficulties, which make it more difficult for

Europeans and Americans to understand this mysterious religion. And terms such as "religion," "liberation," "human being," "self," "soul," "death," and "rebirth" may conjure up concepts completely different within us than in the ancient Indian culture within which Buddhism developed. It would take many lifetimes to study all the Buddhist literature. Many of the thousands of scriptures have more pages than the Bible. In comparison, the "library" for Christians — the Old and the New Testaments — consists of seventy-three books for Catholics and sixty-six for Protestants.

## ✸ With Different Vehicles to Nirvana

Today Buddhism is considered to be the fourth-largest world religion. The estimates of its followers fluctuate between 150 million and 500 million people. It is difficult to determine exact figures because it is possible to be a Buddhist and also belong to another religion. For 1993, the German Statistical Almanac reports that there were 309.1 million Buddhists (5.7 percent of the earth's population) throughout the world. Of these, 307.3 million lived in Asia (9.7 percent of the Asian population). China was home to 67 million Buddhists (5.8 percent of the Chinese population). In Europe, there were about 271,000 Buddhists and in the areas of the former Soviet Union 404,000. There were about 1.1 million in America; 25,000 in Australia and New Zealand; and 20,000 in Africa.

The Buddhists consider their teachings to be like a vehicle into nirvana. This is why the various schools are called the Lesser, the Greater, and the Diamond Vehicles — Hinayana, Mahayana, and Vajrayana. The older school, Hinayana (also called Theravada), is mainly found in Ceylon, Thailand, Burma, and Cambodia today. Mahayana, which developed around 1000 CE, is prevalent in China, Japan, Vietnam, and Korea. Vajrayana can be found in Tibet, Mongolia, and Japan.

## ❀ Between Hinduism and the Modern Age

Essential points of Buddhist teachings are based on the religious and philosophical ideas of the older Hinduism. This applies to the continual cycle of existences and the teachings about karma, according to which good and bad deeds have an effect on future reincarnations. Monasticism also originated before the Buddhist period. The Buddhist community in the narrower sense called *sangha,* is composed of monks (*bhikshu*) and nuns (*bhikshuni*). The Buddha supposedly had some doubts about an order of nuns because he was worried about the morals of the order. For a long time, the nuns had to follow stricter rules than the monks and were subordinate to them. Today, above all in Mahayana, monks and nuns have long been equals. In the larger sense, laypeople also belong to the Buddhist community.

The stringing together of concepts, which is typical for Buddhism, the so-called *Samkhya,* also existed before the time of the Buddha. It is really the oldest complete system of thought in existence. In this process, a concept is determined by listing its components. This creates chains of concepts such as the "Buddhist Credo" and the Four Noble Truths, which are mentioned below. Other practices such as asceticism and yoga were also familiar during the mid-sixth century in northern India.

## The Dalai Lama Is Not a Buddhist Pope

The word "Buddhism" has been used in the modern scientific study of religion as a general term to describe various currents. But the multitude of movements and schools does not have a head. There is no "Buddhist Pope." However, this does not negate the fact that the Dalai Lama, with his humanitarian nature, selflessness, and clarity of thought, embodies Buddhism and the figure of the historical Buddha for the West like no one else.

The term "Buddhism" comes from the word "Buddha" — "The Awakened One" — an honorary title of the historic founder of the religion, Prince Siddhartha Gautama. He lived in the fifth century BCE (ca. 560 to 480 BCE) in what is now the border region of India and Nepal. Because he came from the Sakya tribe, he is also called the Buddha Sakyamuni (the Wise Man from the Tribe of Sakya). According to tradition, he awoke through "his own power" from the night of delusion to the realization of the light. He overcame hatred, greed, and blindness and is worshiped as an exalted but mortal human being. Yet, according to his own statements, he was not the first Buddha, and even more Buddhas were to follow him. In contrast to Jesus Christ, Gautama Buddha saw his role as a guide and not a savior.

In a certain sense, Buddhism has a special position among the religions. It is the oldest religion with a universal outlook. As mentioned above, it does not recognize a god as the creator of the world. The universe and the moral world order have existed since time immemorial. This is why some in the West have called Buddhism an "atheistic religion." However, in later developments, the Buddha was worshiped as divine, although he allegedly rejected this status. Amidism in Japan, with its complete devotion to the Buddha Amida, is very close to monotheism in this sense.

## ❀ All Beings Can Be Liberated

Like no other religion, Buddhist teachings emphasize impermanence. This is why people spoke of "pessimistic Buddhism" for a long time in Europe and used the European affirmation of existence to oppose it as a movement negating the world. But this rather biased perspective has been replaced by deeper insights. Buddhists do not live in negation but point to a path of liberation upon which all beings can overcome the sorrowful "cycle of existences," which is called samsara. It is the Buddhist goal to free all beings from suffering and help them attain the liberation of nirvana (cessation), thereby ending the chain of rebirths.

Human beings are not aware that the life they are chasing brings them the incessant return of suffering, pain, disappointment, loss, age, and death. Knowledgeable persons no longer "attach" their desire to pleasures but constantly strive to do what is right. Neither "what" they live nor even the fact "that (they live)" is essential anymore but rather the "how" of life. The liberation from suffering in all of its forms, nirvana, results on its own through this change in the direction of the will.

## ❀ From Samsara to Nirvana

So the Buddhist strives to move from the cycle of existence, or samsara, to nirvana. What nirvana truly means can be discovered only through intuition, experience, and contemplation — like all of the Indian wisdom teachings — and not just through theory.

In some scriptures, nirvana is seen as a state of bliss that occurs partially in this world and partially beyond this world. In Mahayana Buddhism, nirvana is also understood to be a blissful state, a state of oneness with the Absolute, which occurs after purification from false concepts and desires. Every being bears within itself the potential for becoming a Buddha and attaining perfect enlightenment through its own efforts.

A path to liberation is definitely shown, but there is no savior. Human beings remain dependent upon themselves. However, the "Greater Vehicle" with its bodhisattvas, its beings of enlightenment that also include the Dalai Lama, seems to moderate this statement. This is because the bodhisattvas make the vow to take on the suffering of all beings through active help and transfer their own karmic merits to others. Here the Buddha is one with the Absolute. He manifests himself in our world in order to be able to work for the welfare of all beings.

 ## The "Three Jewels"

Meditation, as well as knowledge and analysis of the Buddhist scriptures, is important for the path of liberation. In order to progress on this path, Buddhists take refuge with their hearts in the "Three Jewels" (*Triratna*): in Buddha, the teacher; in dharma, the teachings; and in *sangha*, the community of companions on the path. "Like someone who has set upright what has fallen over, who uncovers what has been veiled, who shows the lost person the way, or who bring light into the darkness so that it is possible to see, this is how the Exalted One has comprehensively disclosed his teachings. 'Lord, I take refuge in the Exalted One, I take refuge in the teachings, I take refuge in the community of monks,' is how it is written in an ancient text" (A. D. Khoury).

The various forms of meditation and spiritual development that are important in Buddhism are intended to dissolve our "false ego-consciousness." They can be adapted to the possibilities of each person. A distinction is made between an analytical and a deepening meditation.

In the analytical methods, we concentrate on our own self. With attentiveness, we should become aware of obvious things such as our breath or walking. This meditation can be practiced during everyday activities. Through an attitude of observation, we can learn how to think more clearly and act more consciously.

When we have calmed the mind, we hope for a deeper insight into the impermanent and intrinsic nature of life. In the deepening meditation practice, the mind is directed at one single object in order to merge with it. The self, the subject, should become one with the object of the meditation. There are various other states of contemplation that can be achieved through special exercises.

## ❈ Ethics That Also Includes Animals

Above all, Buddhism has a moral aspect with high ethical demands. What is important here is the proper attitude. Because of its radical standards, at the beginning it was a demanding path of liberation for only a few people. Later it developed into a teaching of liberation for the masses. The heart of Buddhist ethics is the demand not to harm anyone in thoughts, words, or actions. It is assumed that all living beings, even the lowest species of animals, want to be happy and do not want to suffer. One of the first

Europeans who truly made the effort to understand Buddhism was Arthur Schopenhauer. He considered Buddhist ethics to be superior to those of Christians because they included animals.

Moral actions are oriented according to five basic commitments:

1. Living beings must not be killed.

2. We should not take anything that is not voluntarily given.

3. We must be in control of the desires of our senses.

4. We must not lie.

5. We must not consume any intoxicating drinks.

In addition, monks must adhere to 253 special rules. For Buddhism, human existence is a step on the path to liberation. The human life is both a task and an opportunity to prove that we are worthy to become purified beings through loving-kindness and active compassion, *karuna*.

## ❀ No "Holy War"

The Western observer is surprised time and again at how tolerantly Buddhism encounters other philosophies and religions. There is no exclusivity. It is possible to be a Buddhist and belong to another religious community at the same time. For example, specific spiritual exercises are not considered elements of the religion and can be adapted to various cultures. However, the general human ideal of moral perfection is obligatory for all. The teachings of the Buddha are available to everyone but should not be forced upon anyone. For many centuries, monks were the only ones permitted to write the texts, if they were expressly requested to do so.

For Christian culture, the commandment "Thou shalt not kill" stands in the forefront. Buddhism goes even further and proclaims: You must not harm other sentient beings. Ahimsa, the principle of "nonharming," also includes animals. All Buddhists are profoundly influenced by this spiritual attitude. In contrast to many other religions, Buddhism has therefore almost always spread without any bloodshed and has become a movement of peace. But it has not remained a completely "untarnished religion." Even in Buddhism, there have been bloody wars and violent deeds in the course of its long history. However, there has never been any religious fanaticism. The concept of a "holy war" is foreign to the Buddha's followers.

A Religion of Common Sense

It is also possible to understand the Buddhist teachings as a method of psychological healing, comparable to psychotherapy, that teaches us how we can master destructive forces like anger, envy, and greed. Human beings seem to be a bundle of different qualities and psychological processes. We should attentively examine our qualities and be alertly aware of our experiences in order to recognize what we truly feel and think. At the same time, the personality of human beings is not seen as a unified whole. According to these teachings, the heart of consciousness is composed of various elements, the five types of attachment, or *skandhas*: body, sensations, perceptions, instinctual forces, and consciousness.

These inner forces impart the false concept of an ego consciousness. The basic problem of emotional disorders therefore lies in a false concept of identity. This I-blindness should therefore be abolished through self-study. Buddhism considers the idea of an eternal soul or self to be a delusion, fundamental ignorance, that must be overcome. The goal is not self-realization but selflessness, emphasizes Gonsar Rinpoche. There are no sharp dividing lines between therapy and religion here.

In Buddhism, the outer circumstances are not made responsible for wrong behavior. As in psychoanalysis, it is presumed that our relationships with the outer world are strongly determined by projections.

## ❀ The Double Face of Religion and Philosophy

Time and again, the question arises whether Buddhism tends to be more of a philosophical system than a religion. It actually does have a double face. On the one side, there are philosophical interpretations — even if every perception that is not directly related to liberation is considered to be superfluous curiosity. Buddhism does not provide answers to metaphysical questions. The other side is the expression of a religious form of life as the bearer of a culture and foundation of radical ethics.

Philosophy and religion are not understood as contrary to each other. They merge into a unity in Buddhist thought and actions. Buddhism is always based on concrete experiences and is a religion of common sense in many ways. There are numerous reports of how the Buddha himself called upon people to sensibly examine his own teachings. The ways of thinking and behaving that he demonstrated are based upon a precise analysis of the world. The Dalai Lama supports the view that knowledge is even more important than belief in his religion. The greatest difference in comparison to Christianity is probably that the Buddha does not demand an act of belief.

## ✿ The Buddha and the Greek Thinkers

The Buddha Sakyamuni is one of the great thinkers of humanity. His teachings coincide with early Greek philosophy in some points. In the same vein as the Buddha, Parmenides (born 540 BCE) announced: "Thinking and being are the same." The distinction made by Alcmaeon of Croton (born 520 BCE), a Greek physician, between transitory sensory perception and thought as a path to the truth is also reminiscent of him. With the Buddha, dialogue as a form of teaching took place for the first time, the conversation between an "I" and a "you." He began his instruction by answering the questions of his students. A parallel to Socrates (born around 470 BCE) can also be found here. He attempted to bring people from all classes to independent thinking through philosophical conversation in order to lead them to the path of truth and virtue.

The well-known Catholic theologian Romano Guardini sees the Buddha Sakyamuni as a challenge for Christian thinking: "There is one single person who could inspire thoughts that come close to those of Jesus: the Buddha. This man is a great mystery. He stands in a frightening, almost superhuman freedom; at the same time, he has a kindness that is as powerful as a world force. Perhaps the Buddha will be the last with whom Christianity has to confront itself. The Buddha's profound observations of reality have lastingly influenced the entire history of the mind."

For the Buddha Sakyamuni, the central questions were these: Why are all beings entangled in a cycle of existence, samsara? Why must they wander through this sorrowful cycle of rebirths countless times? How can they be liberated from it? This cycle of existence occurs according to strict causality in the Buddhist perspective, according to the law of cause and effect: (1) From ignorance arise (2) karma-creating instinctual forces from which come (3) consciousness and then (4) the name and physical form (individual). This is how (5) the senses develop and with them (6) the contact (sensory perceptions) with the outside world. From (7) the sensations, (8) thirst (greed) arises and from it (9) the inclination to life. This results in (10) karmic development, and with it (11) a new birth and (12) again aging and dying.

The famous religious scholar Helmuth von Glasenapp called the concept of the wheel of life an "ancient piece of philosophy, which totally carries the stamp of an archaic way of thinking." Everything that is, is strung together. There is no differentiation between material and other causes. And yet the Buddha's concepts also remind us of the modern holistic view of the world.

The Buddha Sakyamuni came to the conclusion that neither human beings nor the world have a solid existence. All of life consists of compounded manifestations that are all interwoven with each other. He did not recognize imperishable material atoms. The ultimate components from which all existence is composed have the name of dharma. They are neither endowed with a soul nor animated. In this worldview, things are grouped together that we today would certainly divide into various categories: sentient beings ranging from the animals, human beings, spirits, and up to the gods; the elements of water, fire, air, and earth; sounds, senses, sensations, consciousness, and impermanence, as well as hatred, greed, fame, and beauty.

## ❀ Only the Moment is "Real"

Dharma, the smallest particles, are manifest only for a short time and then pass away again. The cosmic law of the world, which is also called dharma, is manifested within them. The entire world is subject to this order. The law

of dharma also controls the karmic rebirths. It simply includes everything. The Buddha offered no explanation on
how the law of karma came about. He did not believe that
metaphysical speculations beyond knowledge were important. He also did not believe in a Creator God who made
everything. The universe has existed from time immemorial. It is a continuum of impermanence. All being flows,
constantly changing. It comes into existence and it passes
away. Life is impermanent, unstable, and "nonintrinsic."
It is *anatman* (no-self).

This view of things also influences the concept of time.
Only this moment is real. Time does not flow from the
past to the present to the future, as we think. Instead,
each of the individual moments takes the place of the last
one in a flash like the second hand of a ticking clock. A
metaphor for this is the way in which the uninterrupted
series of frames in a film deludes us into seeing a relationship between them. The exercises of Zen meditation are
concentrated completely on the "presence of being." The
philosophical essence of Buddhism is that all life is due to
"dependent becoming."

##  Karma Outlasts Death

There is room for neither the soul nor the self in this worldview. As previously mentioned, the soul is composed of a sum of spiritual factors. They manifest themselves in a physical frame and they merge into a new individual. They are created through the law of karma and outlast physical death. The concept of karma is a crucial point of the Buddhist teachings. The karmic forces are compared to the tiny pipal seeds from which a giant tree grows. Every deed produces a "fruit," *phala,* which falls back upon the responsible person. This image is comparable to our concept of the curse of the evil deed. Sayings such as "you reap what you sow" and "life is what you make of it" are based on similar concepts.

The effect of karma can extend across a number of existences. The decisive factor here is the intention behind a deed, which is also the least conspicuous aspect. The human mind creates its own karma. Beneficial actions create joy and happiness, and harmful ones result in trouble and suffering. Good and bad deeds create our legacy, which then becomes the foundation for the coming new life.

Reincarnation means that the deceased person and a newborn, through whom the karmic forces continue to work, are actually two different beings. They are first connected by the "thirst for life" that seeks a new womb instead of letting go of everything in death. It is the force that selects the circumstances and conditions of the new life and creates the form of the reincarnation.

These karmic forces determine whether the next existence will enjoy the amenities of a human or divine existence or will be reincarnated in the lower worlds.

## ✸ About the Double Truth

The school of Madhyamika has had major significance for Mahayana Buddhism and can be traced back to the Indian philosopher Nagarjuna in the second and third centuries.

On the Middle Way we must avoid any deviations to the right or the left and stay away from all apparently irreconcilable opposites.

With his "logic of negation," Nagarjuna wanted to penetrate ignorance step by step with the "Eightfold Path of Negation." He attempted to dialectically disprove opposing opinions. For Nagarjuna, all things exist only through their opposite. This is why they are relative, empty, and nonintrinsic. In his "Teachings of the Double Truth," Nagarjuna distinguished between a "lower" and a "higher" truth. A statement can initially appear to be true from an earlier and limited perspective but can become only a partial truth or even be wrong from a later and higher view. A = common truth, B = higher truth; this becomes from a higher viewpoint AB = lower truth, C = higher truth. The pair of opposites can in turn become a lower truth from a higher perspective. In this manner, we attain an increasingly comprehensive view of the truth. This is how we can grasp the worldview of modern physics in comparison to Newtonian concepts as a more comprehensive view of the world and a "higher truth" in the Buddhist sense.

A statement can be seen as true in the short term, but appear to be untrue in the long run. Truth in the highest sense is free of multiplicity, and all opposites are suspended. It exists beyond yes or no, beyond any tangible statement, and is identical with the complete void. This void, *shunyata*, has two aspects to it. On the one hand, it means the emptiness of a "self"; on the other hand, it means being liberated. Once this void has been realized, we are liberated from everything.

Only when the mind stands above all things has it been purified of every assent or negation. In a certain sense, the Middle Way tricks us. Even though nothing exists, we live with great commitment. Toward the outside, we accept the world with its suffering as if it really existed, even though we have experienced its emptiness. As a result, we commit ourselves to the rules of morality and want to help ourselves and others progress on the path of liberation because of compassion. The Dalai Lama expressed it in this way: "Things basically do not exist at all, but because we now have come into this existence we should make the best of it."

## ✸ A Prince Chooses Homelessness

Like Christianity and Islam, Buddhism also has a historical founder, Gautama Siddhartha Buddha, as discussed above. The father of the historical Buddha was Suddhodana and his mother was Maya. Both came from the warrior caste of Sakya. Gautama was born in 566 or 563 BCE. and received the proper name of Siddhartha (He Who Has Reached His Goal). His mother died several weeks after his birth, and Gautama was raised by his sister Mahaprajapati. Since Suddhodana was the elected regent of the Republic of Sakya, the legend arose that Gautama led the luxurious life of a royal prince. However, Buddhologists believe that even the young Buddha enjoyed learning and was aware of his responsibilities (Volker Zotz). The impermanence of all things increasingly became the dominant impression for him.

Legend has woven this inner development into a series of external experiences. During four consecutive outings, Siddhartha encountered a deity in various forms: as a frail and trembling old man, as a diseased person shaking with fever, as a decomposing corpse, and finally as an ascetic, a homeless wanderer. The ascetic's serene facial expression showed that he had been elevated above the misery of impermanence.

At the age of sixteen, Gautama married Yashodhara. After the birth of his son, Rahula, he left his family and chose to be "homeless" at the age of twenty-nine. At first, he joined various ascetic teachers. Then he attempted to attain liberation from sorrowful existence, samsara, in great solitude through extreme fasting and dangerous breathing exercises.

After six years of seeking in vain, he came to the insight that he would not reach his goal in this way. He ended this life of deprivation and turned to meditation. Gautama recuperated on the shores of the Nairanjana. There, in the area surrounding the village that is now known as Bodh-Gaya, in the Indian state of Bihar, he sat down under a fig tree, sometimes called the Bo tree. After many weeks of meditation, he achieved "perfect enlightenment," the "awakening," *Bodhi*, at the age of thirty-five. He had liberated himself. He discovered the Middle

Way, the avoidance of extremes between debauchery and asceticism.

According to Buddhist tradition, he recalled his previous forms of existence during this time and recognized the reincarnation of other beings. He attained the knowledge of the Four Noble Truths, namely, how the three basic evils of sensory desire, the desire to become, and ignorance can be ended. As H. von Glasenapp describes it, "In the Liberated One is the liberation. Rebirth has ceased, and the sacred change is completed. What had to be done has been done. After this life, there are no more." So he left the cycle of rebirths and attained nirvana in this life. Because he did not know whether he could truly impart the experience of enlightenment to others, he initially decided to remain silent about it.

## ✸ Dharma-Chakra, the Wheel of Teaching

Only the urgent pleas of his followers made Siddhartha Gautama move from place to place as a teacher and helper until the time of his death. The band of followers — monks, nuns, and laypeople whom he convinced about his path of liberation — continually grew. These words have been attributed to him: "Like the great ocean is permeated by just one taste, the taste of salt, this teaching and this order is permeated by just one taste, the taste of liberation." According to legend, the "Enlightened One" passed away into *parinirvana,* a complete ceasing to exist, in the arms of his favorite student, Ananda, at the age of eighty after a case of food poisoning.

In his sermon at Sarnath near Benares in 528 BCE, the Buddha set the "Wheel of Teaching" in motion. A wheel with eight spokes symbolizes the teachings of the Buddha. This image means that the teachings of the Buddha will be in effect during the age of this world as long as the wheel turns. If it stops, a new Buddha, the future Buddha Maitreya, will appear. The Buddha Sakyamuni first proclaimed the basis of his teaching, the Four Noble Truths, to five wandering ascetics.

His approach followed a method of healing, *Samkhya,* which comes from an ancient Indian form of stringing things together:

1. The diagnosis of the evil: all life is suffering.

2. Finding the cause: all suffering has its roots in desire, in "thirst."

3. Eliminating the cause: the stopping of this desire leads to the cessation of suffering, to interrupting the chain of rebirths.

4. The means to use for this purpose: the path of liberation is the sacred Eightfold Path, namely, right
   belief, right thinking, right speech, right actions,
   right living, right striving, right thoughts, and right
   contemplation.

## ✤ Buddhism Becomes a World Religion

The Buddha directed his message to all people, without
any exceptions. This is, as it were, a move to universal
humanity and away from the strict ascetic practices of
this originally "aristocratic" religion. Its first followers also
came mainly from the upper class. Above all, it is due
to the Indian emperor Ashoka (246 BCE) with his "government of dharma" that Buddhist teachings spread from
India, and Buddhism became a world religion.

As with the life of Jesus, there are no eyewitness reports
of the life of Gautama. The oral traditions were collected
several centuries after the death of Gautama Buddha. In a
number of councils, the sacred scriptures were combined
into a canon. At the same time, there were far-reaching
differences in opinion about the authenticity of the numerous collections of scriptures that led to divisions into
various currents and sects.

The "Greater Vehicle" of Mahayana was written in the first century BCE. It was compared with the older school, the so-called "Lesser Vehicle" of Hinayana. The word "vehicle" (*yana*) is a metaphor. The teachings are understood to be a vehicle with which we can get to the "safe shore," nirvana. From the perspective of Mahayana, the vehicle of the older school appears to be small because it offers room for only a single person seeking liberation, the arhat. This liberation is based solely on the individual's own efforts here. There is space for everyone in the "Greater Vehicle." All beings should attain liberation. The ideal of the arhat was replaced by the concept of the bodhisattva. The "Diamond Vehicle," the Vajrayana, arose in the middle of the first millennium from the encounter with Hindu tantrism and reached Tibet together with Mahayana.

## ❀ A Change of Paradigm

With the Mahayana, a change of paradigm from an elite religion to a religion of the masses occurred in Buddhism. Because people cannot survive for long without prayer, ritual, or a belief in miracles, much of what was discarded managed to find its way back in. Buddhism had to come to the realization that its teaching about liberation, which consciously renounced every cult, did not satisfy the longings of the masses. So the simple garment of asceticism was transformed into a splendidly colored, sumptuous robe. Numerous customs of various cultures have found their way into it. But the Buddhist teaching, the dharma, has remained unchanged at its core.

A far-reaching transformation began at this point. Buddhism began to be a church. Less value was placed upon the monastic life, and even laypeople could realize nirvana. The Buddha was worshipped like a god and the heavens were populated with many other Buddhas, even though Gautama Buddha had expressly rejected the concept of a god from whom we could experience help.

The many transcendent Buddhas are intended to embody various aspects of the Buddha. The Buddha principle is primarily manifested in the "Three Bodies," *Trikaya*. The concept of the "Pure Land" also emerges. In Buddhist teaching, these are "aspects of enlightened consciousness." The popular belief sees it as Paradise and hopes to be reborn there. The help of the Buddha is decisive in this process. Even the deities, who ensure protection against threatening demons, are basically nothing other than a pure emanation of the individual's own consciousness. But pious people pray to them for help in a way similar to the way the saints are called upon in the Catholic Church.

## ✺ The Teachings of the Buddha Come to Tibet

The first contacts of Buddhism with Tibet took place in the seventh century CE. The result was a blending of the pre-Buddhist Bön religion — a nature religion with shamanic elements such as rainmaking, magic formulas, and exorcisms — and the teachings of the Buddha. Tradition attributes the introduction of Buddhism to King Trisong Detsen (755–797) and his two wives, a Chinese princess and a Nepalese princess. The two princesses are also embodied in the Green and the White Tara, a popular deity. Buddhism was declared the official religion and supplanted the old Bön religion. The Bön religion is probably what gave Tibet its name; the Tibetans call their country *Böd* and themselves *Bödpa* after it.

According to historical sources, the Indian tantric Padmasambhava is considered to be the founder of Tibetan Buddhism. Instead of battling the old deities, he included them in the Buddhist worldview. Legend says that he banned the demonic forces that resist the Buddhist dharma and transformed them into the protective powers of Buddhism. Around 755, he founded the first monastery in Samye.

The situation of Buddhism fluctuated during the Middle Ages. During the ninth century, it was persecuted for political reasons. In the eleventh century, it was revived again. Four main schools of Tibetan Buddhism developed. The oldest is the school of Nyingmapa, which came from Padmasambhava. As a follower of Mahayana, the Indian Athisa attempted to enforce the rule of the Buddhist order. The school of Kadampa emerged from this reform. The other schools are Kagyupa and Sakayapa. The abbots of the Sakayapa make up the central leading authority.

 ## The Great Fifth

After another phase of decline, the reform by Master Tsongkhapa took place in the fourteenth century. This is when the large monasteries of Gaden, Drepung, and Sera were established. Tashilumpo was built sometime later. Tibetan Buddhism spread in the neighboring regions as far as Mongolia and Siberia. Tsongkhapa is also the founder of the Gelugpa School, the "Yellow Church."

In the sixteenth century, Sonam Gyatso, who later was the Third Dalai Lama, helped the Gelugpas experience a major upswing. He converted the Mongolian ruler Altan Khan to Buddhism and, in 1578, received from him the title of Dalai Lama, which means "teacher whose wisdom is as great as the ocean." In order to secure his position, both of his predecessors were awarded the title posthumously. The "Great Fifth" was the beginning of the Gelugpas' rulership over all of Tibet. The "Fifth" installed the Panchen Lama as the second spiritual power and had the Potala Palace built in Lhasa as a residence.

In the late seventeenth century, Buddhism had already grown deep roots in its Tibetan form in the Land of Snow. Tibetan Buddhism also spread throughout Mongolia, where it has survived to this day. It penetrated into the bordering Chinese province of Yünnan and reached the Indian Himalayan regions of Ladakh, Lahual, Spiti, Sikkim, and Arunachal Pradesh through Nepal and Bhutan.

## ✺ The Sangha Influences the Society

In the course of time, the influence of the monasteries with their temples, monastic cities, and universities consistently increased in Tibet. The entire societal structure was influenced by the model of the Buddhist *sangha*. Almost all of the land belonged to the nobility or the monasteries. The political power was also in the hands of these two classes. All the important offices were occupied by aristocrats or monks.

"I was now at the head of a system of government that is unique but hopelessly outdated and, unfortunately, also pervaded with corruption after so many years of rule. For example, it was not unusual for the top positions to be sold," the Dalai Lama wrote in his biography.

Even at the beginning of the twentieth century, there were almost five hundred thousand monks and nuns in Tibet out of a total population of approximately five million. Complicated hierarchical systems had developed to regulate monastic life and the many ceremonies and prayer gatherings. The monasteries were divided into various departments and subdepartments. Some movements placed more weight on studies while others focused on spiritual development and meditation for the monks.

All the monasteries were supported by voluntary donations of money, grain, and butter from the laypeople. In return, they attended to the religious life of the Tibetans. Mahayana had the Buddhist *dana* system, which recognized the voluntary giving of material things or spiritual goods as an important virtue for the path of enlightenment. When a person gives something, that person thanks the receiver because the receiver has helped the giver to do a good deed.

## Not Lamaism

Because of the special role of the lamas, Tibetan Buddhism is also called Lamaism. The Dalai Lama has continually pointed out that this term is misleading. Tibetan Buddhism is part of Mahayana and follows the traditional texts. The Tibetan word "lama" has the same meaning as the Sanskrit word "guru," which is more common in the West. They both mean a spiritual leader who shows the "path of liberation." The lamas are shown special veneration because they embody Buddhist teachings. Their traditional training includes years of studies. A person can become a lama only after three years of seclusion and is then permitted to pass his knowledge on to others. Special masters are awarded the honorary title of "Rinpoche."

The *Tibetan Book of the Dead* from the fourteenth century has been very well known in the West for decades. In Tibetan, it is called the *Bardo Thödröl* (liberation through hearing in the intermediate state). It should be studied during one's lifetime so that one can become familiar with the various tasks of the Buddhas, deities, and demons that people are said to encounter after they die. If death has occurred, the monks use a specific ritual to explain to the spirit of the deceased what happens to it when it wanders

about during the forty-nine days in *Bardo*, in the intermediate state. The spirit is warned against letting itself
be tempted into a rebirth by various rays of light and
manifestations. Only when the spirit has gathered enough
good karma will it be able to go into nirvana from this
intermediate state.

## ✸ Tulkus and Other Enlightened Beings

Tibetan Buddhists believe that the great lamas return
again after their death. Through their bodhisattva vows
they have obligated themselves not to remain in nirvana
but to continue to work for the good of all beings. There
is a precise procedure for recognizing these enlightened
beings: their words and ethical behavior are put to the
test, omens of their birth are sought, and oracles are questioned. Many lamas can still remember the details of their
previous life. A high-ranking lama determines whether the
reincarnation is genuine. There were supposedly about ten
thousand reincarnated lamas, especially in Tibet, before
1959. Since the exile, the figure is about four hundred
throughout the world. According to Gonsar Rinpoche,
there are many little Rinpoches in the Buddhist monasteries of India. He explained this by saying that many high

lamas lost their lives during the 1960s under Chinese rule and have now returned together.

As a famous example from the present, the Buddhists mention the reincarnation of Geshe Rapten, the spiritual adviser to the Dalai Lama, who died in 1985. The Tenzin Rabgyä was found in Dharamsala by the abbot of the monastery on Lake Geneva, Gonsar Rinpoche. He is growing up in seclusion on the Swiss Mont Pélerin (Mountain of the Pilgrims) at the only Tibetan monastery in Europe. Here both Tibetan and European monks can study Buddhist philosophy and learn Tibetan together. Visitors who participate in the impressive religious festivals that are celebrated here feel like they have been transported to Tibet.

Some lamas are given the name *tulku* (body of transformation). In earlier times, the various *tulku* lineages were an especially important means of ensuring the spiritual and political successors in the monasteries. The *tulkus* are also subjected to a series of tests before they are recognized as such.

## ❀ Flawless Like a Diamond

A special feature of Tibetan Buddhism is the merging of ancient Indian monastic rules with the various cults of the "Diamond Vehicle," the Vajrayana. This vehicle is linked with the "Greater Vehicle" and has integrated elements of Indian tantrism. The minds of Buddhist students should become as flawless as diamonds. Tantras are esoteric texts on astrology, medicine, and religion. They supposedly date back to the historical Buddha Sakyamuni. It is obvious that a master is required for an introduction to the tantras. Only when the lama considers someone to be mature enough does he make this person his student through a special rite *(Abhisheka)*.

The texts are intended to be understood intuitively, based on experience. They describe, for example, the various levels of spiritual ascent. The tantric school believes that the truth cannot be comprehended with the rational mind alone. As a result, the tantric practices are also related to the mind, language, and body. In Hinduism, this approach is used for uniting with cosmic energy; in Buddhism, it leads to the wisdom of the Buddha.

## ❁ Mantras are Sacred Syllables

In Tibetan Buddhism there are also sumptuous cults and an ever-present belief in demons and magic. People circumambulate religious shrines, setting prayer wheels in motion, and the priest holds a prayer scepter, *vadjra*, in his hands. The use of holy formulas, called mantras; and meditation aids in picture form, the mandalas, as well as

the rituals related to magic, called *mudra,* all come from
the Hindu tantra. With these aids, people hope to shorten
the path to nirvana. The ancient magical practices appear much like psychological methods for transforming
consciousness.

Because the mantras are so well received by people,
the Buddhism of Tibet is also called Mantrayana. Mantras
are power-charged "sacred syllables" that express certain
cosmic forces and aspects of the Buddha and protect the
mind.

During meditation, a person visualizes the various
manifestations of the Buddha and constantly repeats the
mantras at the same time. The most familiar Tibetan
mantra is the six-syllable phrase *om mani peme (padme)
hum.* For Tibetan Buddhists, it expresses the basic attitude of compassion and the desire for liberation. This is
reminiscent of the "Prayer of the Heart" in the Ortho-
dox Church, in which people desire to become one with
God in their hearts through the continual "remembrance
of God."

## ✸ About Hungry Ghosts and Flying Palaces

In Buddhist cosmology, the "mythological world mountain of Meru" stands at the center of the universe. It is

surrounded by oceans and continents. Beneath it are the "cold and hot" hells and the realm of the "hungry ghosts." The various gods in their "flying palaces" live above it.

The "hungry ghosts," *pretas*, have giant stomachs but mouths that are only the size of the eye of a needle; as a result, they must suffer the painful torment of hunger. People can become hungry ghosts if they were miserly, envious, or jealous during their lifetimes.

An endless series of worlds being created and worlds dying follow each other. There is neither lasting deterioration nor infinite progress; instead, the rise and fall follow each other. In the various ages of the world, the lifespan decreases from eighty thousand years to ten years and then slowly increases back to eighty thousand years. People ask how the Buddha Sakyamuni could have attained a concept of such infinitely large dimensions without modern astronomical insights. Where a person is born, into which cultural surroundings and which world system, depends completely on that person's respective karma.

 ## The Wheel of Life

The mythological concept of the transmigration of souls is frequently illustrated as the "Wheel of Life" on the Tibetan *tanka*. This is a picture that depicts the closed system of

Buddhist psychology. The threatening demon Yama, the Judge of the Dead, usually holds a circle with six wedge-shaped divisions in his claws. Each area corresponds to one level of the cycle of existence. There is the area of the gods, the anti-gods (titans), the humans, the animals, the hungry ghosts, and the hell beings. The gods, *suras* or *devas*, live in a splendid palace. The crown of the "Wish-Fulfilling Tree" is found in their area. The Buddha appears with a lute that reminds us of impermanence.

This is followed by the world of the *asuras*, the anti-gods. Their life is a constant battle, and their main characteristic is envy. They want to take the fruits of the "Wish-Fulfilling Tree" for themselves. The Buddha appears with a sword, the symbol of wisdom. He reminds people to strive for inner peace instead of power and money.

The world of human beings with age, illness, and death is connected to the heavenly realm. The Buddha appears with a bowl for alms and a walking stick, an indication of impermanence. The three lower realms are occupied by the animals, the hungry ghosts, and the hell beings. Animals have no knowledge of the freedom of human beings. The Buddha appears with a book and points to the liberating power of thought. The hungry ghosts must learn to be generous to each other.

The Buddha carries a vessel with *amrita,* the nectar of the gods. The hell beings must suffer horrible torments that remind us of Dante's *Inferno.* The cold and hot hells symbolize the various forms of hatred. The Buddha appears here with a cleansing flame, the symbol of purification, so that even the destructive soul forces can be transformed into beneficial inner gifts.

The "Wheel of Life" is just one example of the variety and special characteristics of Tibetan Buddhism. The abundance of Tibet's sacred scriptures is apparent in the following figures. The Tibetan canon includes more than three hundred volumes, containing all the Buddhist works that have been translated into Tibetan from the original Sanskrit. The *Kangyur* contains the collection of all the instructions given by the Buddha Sakyamuni. It consists of 92 volumes with 1055 texts. The various commentaries, 3,626 in all, are compiled in the 224 volumes of the *Tengyur.*

## ✸ The Radiant Sun of Freedom

Even in Tibet, there was a danger that Buddhism would fragment into hostile sects. But fortunately, the clashes were exhausted in the conflicts over the teachings without causing any confessional divisions. Many lamas are instructed by more than one school. There is no fear of contact between the different schools as in Christianity. The question usually is how philosophical concepts can be combined with the practice. The *Rime* movement arose in the nineteenth century. Its focus is eliminating sectarian tendencies while allowing each school to maintain its independence.

Even after more than thirty years of Chinese rule, after the destruction of more than six thousand monasteries — some of which were the size of a city — Tibet is still one of the most religious countries in the world. As the embodiment of this religiousness, the Dalai Lama continues to enjoy the highest veneration. The Tibetan national flag, which was designed by the Thirteenth Dalai Lama (1876– 1933) and is prohibited today, also shows how much the many-faceted Tibetan form of the Buddha's teachings has been accepted in the life of this people. The white mountains on the flag represent Tibet, the Land of Snow. The twelve red and blue rays are the six mythological original tribes from which the twelve tribes of Tibet originated. Red and blue are the colors of the Tibetan tutelary gods.

The radiant sun at the center symbolizes the hope of freedom, happiness, and affluence. The two mythic lions in the foreground embody the spiritual and the worldly powers. In their paws they hold three flaming jewels, the

"Three Buddhist Jewels" *(Triratna)*, symbolizing the refuge in the Buddha, in dharma, his teachings, and in *sangha*, the community of monks. The lower jewel reminds the Tibetans to uphold ethical demands, and the golden edge indicates the lastingness of Buddhist teachings.

## ✹ Days of Fear, Nights of Mourning

The following words also came from the Thirteenth Dalai Lama. He wrote them in 1932, and they read like a prophecy regarding the coming fate of his people: "It may happen that here in the center of Tibet, religion and government will be attacked both from without and from within. Unless we can guard our own country, it will happen that the Dalai Lama and Panchen Lama, the father and the son, and all the glorious reincarnations, will be degraded and become nameless. The rule of law will be weakened. The lands and other possessions of the monasteries and monks will be seized. They themselves will be forced to serve their enemies or wander the country like beggars. All beings will sink into great hardship and overpowering fear; the days and nights will drag on slowly in suffering."

The dimension of misery and suffering in which these people have had to live for more than forty years is overwhelming. The Chinese marched into Tibet in 1950. The Dalai Lama went into exile in 1959. Between 1950 and 1980, one-sixth of the entire Tibetan population, which means more than one million Tibetans, have lost their lives as a result of this invasion: 175,000 were killed in prison, 156,000 died in mass executions, 413,000 starved during the "Agricultural Reforms," 92,000 were tortured to death, and 10,000 committed suicide.

More than 6,100 monasteries have reportedly been destroyed. As a result, the Tibetans have lost their religious centers. Because of the Communist agricultural reforms and the mismanagement that followed them, famines occurred for the first time in the history of Tibet, natural resources have been plundered; many species of animals and plants have been wiped out; and the environment has been endangered by nuclear waste dumps. Nuclear missiles are now stationed in the former "peace zone." As a result of Beijing's resettlement policies the situation is that the Chinese are now in the majority with 7.5 million people compared to 6 million Tibetans in the country. Despite its size of 2.5 million square kilometers (approximately as large as all of Western Europe), Tibet seems to have been at the edge of world affairs. It has primarily been the appearances and untiring efforts of the Dalai Lama in foreign countries and those of the numerous Tibet organizations that have awakened international interest in the suppressed nation.

## ✿ Reincarnation Breaks through All Barriers

Western authors like to write about old Tibet using the words "feudal" and "theocratic." But neither of these terms can simply be applied to the Buddhist social order. The concept of reincarnation is also completely beyond European understanding. It breaks through the hierarchical structures and becomes a force of balancing justice. Today we would perhaps say that, unlike in Western thought, here there is no distinction between being given an equal opportunity to do something and being judged on how well the thing was done. A better place in life, whether as a *tulku* or as an aristocrat, is not inherited coincidentally. It is earned by individuals themselves through good deeds in a previous life.

Despite its high ideals, Tibet was not free of injustices, corruption, and abuses. Striving for liberation is a powerful motive for economic actions, according to the American sociologist Melford E. Spiro in agreement with Max Weber. With slight irony, he adds that instead of spending so much money on unnecessary gifts to the monks (he is thinking of Burma here), the people could have used it to improve the social services and the school system.

The so-called "original" Buddhism was actually rediscovered by Western intellectuals. But there are very few points of contact with the political ideologies of the West. The teachings of the Buddha are not concerned with changing the state and the societal order. The major goal is solely liberation from a sorrow-filled earthly existence and efforts toward peace among human beings. However, a specific exception to this is the encounter with Marxism. Since 1948, there have been repeated attempts to find a common denominator for the two teachings. This, of course, is not at all related to "real, existing socialism," as it developed in the former Soviet Union and still survives in China today. Instead, the debate is more concerned with Marxism as a comprehensive worldview that raises the claim of radically changing society.

A peculiarity of Tibetan Buddhism is consultation with oracles before making important political decisions. A new Nechung medium was appointed for this purpose in 1987. One of the deities who was called upon during this ritual was Dorje Shudgen. Even though the Dalai Lama had originally followed this tradition himself and his personal teacher had initiated many lamas into the Shudgen cult, the worship of this deity was prohibited some years ago by

Dharamsala. In the following period, there were conflicts between the followers of the oracle god Oeddhar and the worshipers of Shudgen.

Tibetan observers believe that the oracle itself had stirred up this rift and made Shudgen the scapegoat for all evil. The conflict culminated in violent confrontations. The homes of Shudgen followers were supposedly searched by their religious opponents, believers were attacked, and images and altars of the deity were destroyed. The Tibetan government in exile has exerted pressure on the monasteries of the Shudgen tradition and demanded a written dissociation from this cult. Monks who refused to do this were declared traitors. In February of 1997, lama Lobsang Gyatso, who was friends with the Dalai Lama and a vocal opponent of the Shudgen sect, was murdered. It also appears that infiltrating Chinese agents have sowed the seeds of discord and dissension among the people of the Dalai Lama.

Gonsar Rinpoche, the abbot of the Tibetan monastery on Lake Geneva, comments critically: "Today we are experiencing one of the most difficult phases of our history, from which all Tibetans suffer. Yet we must admit that Tibet is a nation like other countries, and the Tibetans are also fallible people. There are no paradisiacal circumstances in this world. In the past, our people have almost always been praised. But too much uncritical praise is not good for anyone. In reality, it is the same in Tibet as anywhere else." In old Tibet there were corrupt officials and scheming monks at the court of some of the Dalai Lamas, and even assassinations reportedly occurred. Among the lamas who appear in the West, there are also charlatans and gurus who are involved in dubious affairs.

 ## The Just Society

Like Buddhists, Marxists do not recognize an almighty Creator God. They want, as they say, to analyze reality scientifically. In this point, they appear to think in a way similar to Buddhists. The ancient Buddhist kingdom did not acknowledge private ownership of land because the sole owner was the state, represented by the king. In the application of the teachings of the "Double Truth" developed by the Buddhist philosopher Nagarjuna, modern Buddhists see Marxism as the "lower" and Buddhism as the "higher" truth.

The "lower" Marxist truth should serve to create a just society that equals the Buddhist ideal state. A classless society also develops through reincarnation because it overcomes all political, social, and national barriers.

Through it, humanity should become one big universal community that approaches the Marxist ideal.

When questioned about his political views, the Dalai Lama says he continues to be a "socialist" in the field of economics. During the 1950s, he once even wanted to become a member of China's Communist Party. In his biography, *Freedom in Exile*, he writes: "The more I became involved with Marxism, the more it appealed to me. Here was a social system based on equality and justice for all that promised to be the universal remedy for all the evils of the world." He sees the only theoretical disadvantage of Marxism in the "purely materialistic understanding of human existence." Even today, he is still convinced that a synthesis between Buddhism and Marxism is possible "from which to develop an effective approach to political action."

## ✸ Violence and Nonviolence

A fundamental difference between Buddhism and Marxism is certainly in the question of the use of violence. Ahimsa, foregoing every type of violence, and revolutionary theory can hardly be united with each other. According to the Marxist concept, the world is not harmonious but antagonistic. The only way to overcome injustice is through the class struggle. Buddhists have reservations about revolting against socially unjust circumstances because, based on the teaching of reincarnation, they assume that they are to blame for the injustice they are experiencing. By rebelling against the injustice, they would again be burdened with guilt in the next life. However, this has changed since the mid-1980s. The Tibetans, who were a warlike people in pre-Buddhist times, have tried in vain to defend themselves in various revolts to which the Chinese put a bloody end.

By Huitzi believes that the theory of nonviolence cannot ultimately be maintained. In the case of Tibet, it is obviously hoped that the Chinese ruling powers can be forced to retreat because of increasing political chaos. It appears to Huitzi that the profession of nonviolence is the hope of the weak who themselves have no army. Others should conduct war. He sees a similar contradictory attitude in the fact that Tibetans themselves do not kill animals but like to buy meat from non-Buddhist butchers.

Quite independent of ahimsa, there are other very realistic reasons for the Dalai Lama to hold on to the principle of nonviolence in the conflict with China. It is clear to him that even the most courageous Tibetans cannot achieve anything against the Chinese ruling powers. It certainly moved him profoundly, as he wrote in his biography, to hear about the death-defying courage of the Tibetan free-dom fighters in 1958 as they attacked superior Chinese military forces.

## ✸ Schopenhauer, the "Buddhist"

For centuries, Europe has had only a very vague con-cept of Buddhism. The initial, still imprecise knowledge about Buddhists came from Jesuit missionaries. In Ger-many, Godfried Wilhelm Leibniz (1646–1716) was the first to look into Buddhist teachings; however, he falsely interpreted some of Buddhism's elements. Martin Bau-mann thinks that not only Leibniz but also subsequent thinkers and poets from Kant to Nietzsche were subject to many misunderstandings because of sparse sources. They all interpreted Buddhism as a doctrine about "Nothing" that was mainly concerned with "suffering."

However, through the writings of Arthur Schopenhauer (1788–1860), who called himself a Buddhist, increasingly larger circles started to become interested in the teachings of the Buddha. Schopenhauer believed that the Buddhist scriptures confirmed his own views. He was supposedly also the first German to set up a statue of the Buddha in his house. At the beginning of the twentieth century, an independent "German Buddhology" developed in academic circles. Later the German Buddhist Society was formed.

So the first Buddhists in Germany were Germans and not Asians. They made the effort to find the "original teachings" of the Buddha within the extensive the Buddhist scriptures. For them, the written word was decisive. Buddhism appeared to them to be a "religion of common sense and humanity," which they contrasted with a Christianity that had become dogmatic. Philosophers, artists, and writers emphasize the ethical Buddhist worldview and the deep teaching of wisdom. On the other hand, religious leaders and politicians speak of a "devastating nihilism" and a "bleak pessimism."

## ✸ A New Buddhist Beginning?

In 1952, the Arya Maitreya Mandala Order (AMM) settled in Germany. It was founded in 1933 by the German Lama Anagarika Govinda (L. E. Hoffmann). The order is not related to any historical Buddhist school but intends to bring a future-oriented Buddhism to the West. This is why it refers especially to the Buddha Maitreya, who is still to come, and hopes for the "great opportunity of a Buddhist new beginning in the West." With the help of

Buddhist religious practices, all people should be able to experience "universal consciousness."

Above all, Lama Govinda wanted to unite the crucial points of the various schools with each other. Since 1958, the German Buddhist Union (DBU) has represented all the Buddhist societies Germany.

In 1991, there were a total of twenty-seven organizations and groups. To date, the Asians have not joined the DBU. There are currently about twenty thousand German and forty thousand Asian Buddhists in Germany.

During the 1960s, a Zen boom occurred in the United States, which has also had an effect on Germany. The writings and psychological interpretations of Zen Buddhism by D. T. Suzuki, Erich Fromm, and C. G. Jung became well known. Books by the Jesuit H. M. Enoymia-Lassalle, as well as those by Karlfried Graf von Dürckheim, awakened interest in Zen meditation. With the hippie movement, "Beat Zen" and an enthusiasm for everything Indian came into fashion. In the 1970s and 1980s, more and more groups developed that were no longer concerned with political change in society like the revolutionaries of the 1960s. Instead, they were interested in their own spiritual life.

##  Tibet and Europe

After the flight of the Dalai Lama and other high Tibetan dignitaries in 1959, Tibetan Buddhism also began to spread in Germany. During the 1950s the Austrian Heinrich Harrer, with his impressive descriptions of his seven-year stay in Tibet, awakened a lively sympathy in Europe for the distant Himalayan nation. In 1966, the Dalai Lama sent Lobsang Dargay to Munich to look after the Mongolian Kalmück Geshe.

In 1968 the monastic Tibetan Institute in Rikon was established by Geshe Rabten, the personal adviser to the Dalai Lama for the approximately one thousand Tibetans who live in Swiss exile. He directed it up until his death in 1986. Because the Tibetans are simple and adaptable people, it was possible for them to acclimate themselves in Switzerland and still preserve their own tradition. The young Tibetans have greater difficulties with this. They frequently do not speak Tibetan and must be instructed in it in special summer courses on Mont Pélerin. Of the approximately five hundred Tibetans who have been adopted by Swiss families, some have even become addicted to drugs and there have been a few cases of suicide. In 1973, the Dalai Lama traveled to Europe himself for the first time. In the 1970s, the lamas also began founding Tibetan centers in Germany and holding lectures. The gloriously colorful and melodious devotional ceremonies especially attract young, educated people.

Martin Baumann believes that Germany has been particularly interested in Buddhist philosophy since the beginning of the twentieth century. In the 1960s, an increasing involvement with meditation arose as well. As a result, the interest was first primarily focused on the "Lesser Vehicle," followed by the "Greater Vehicle." In recent years the Tibetan "Diamond Vehicle" has been well received.

During the 1980s, the Buddhist groups in Germany began to bring their worldview into the environmental movement. They criticized — as did others — the behavior of the consumer society as "desires that underlie blindness" and demanded the "radical personal responsibility of the individual." Especially the factory approach to mass maintenance of animals and vivisection are particularly incompatible with Buddhist ethics, which considers human beings and animals to be equals.

## ✾ Crisis of Meaning in the West

The great response that the Buddhist teachings have met with in Europe and America is a sign of the growing exchange between cultures. But the great interest in Buddhism also reflects the spiritual crisis of the West. The roots of this crisis can be followed back to the Age of Enlightenment. In the nineteenth century, Schopenhauer's pessimistic worldview impressed many of his contemporaries. He was convinced of the meaninglessness of world history and triggered a truly pessimistic wave in European literature. Schopenhauer said "no" to the will to live and, influenced by Buddhism, longed for nirvana. Today however we know that his Buddhist concepts did not exactly correspond with the teachings of Gautama.

Nietzsche saw this nihilism coming in *The Will to Power* a hundred years ago. "What does nihilism mean?" he asked and responded: "That the uppermost values become invalid. The goal is lacking. The answer to the question of 'why' is missing.... The entire idealism of humanity up to now is about to shift into nihilism — into the belief in absolute worthlessness, which is meaninglessness."

After World War II, a strongly materialistic way of thinking asserted itself and further intensified the spiritual crisis. In our affluent society, with its individualism and subjectivism, its longings and dreams of self-realization, there is an increasing feeling of emptiness and meaninglessness. "We are suffering today from a 'neurotic form of nihilism' that expresses itself in alcoholism, drug addiction, and criminality," according to Wolfgang Kraus. A hectic pace, stress, and isolation are continually increasing within the masses of our society.

## A Supermarket for Sects

The Christian church hardly appears to take on this challenge and counter it with an inner renewal. In addition, there is also an anti-institutional attitude toward the churches, which began with the revolution of the 1960s. Even though the "new religious sects" are not very important in terms of their numbers, they increase the impression of a "hyper-offer of possibilities in the supermarket of religions and sects." Religious identification becomes more difficult as a result. "There are people who simultaneously belong to a Catholic congregation, participate in transcendental meditation, and follow horoscopes," according to Roland Campiche, a Protestant philosopher of social ethics from Lausanne, in a conversation with the author.

Many sects with new leaders and gurus take advantage of these feelings of insecurity. To their followers who are looking for the meaning of life, they promise orientation and self-realization through supposedly "new esoteric teachings." This huge "syncretic concoction" also likes to borrow from Tibetan Buddhism with its tantras and mantras. Gonsar Rinpoche, the head of the spiritual center on Mont Pélerin, has this opinion: "Such things are not very useful and are not at all related to serious spiritual development. For us, the most important thing is ethics and not esotericism."

Many people feel lonely and deserted in our mass society. They let themselves be lured by such sects with a supposedly intimate group feeling. But often the price for a "soul trip into happiness" is complete dependence and separation from family and friends. In some cases, the followers even suffer serious emotional harm as a result. Because there are constant attempts to equate the "new religious movements" with Buddhism, the Buddhists have repeatedly had to distinguish themselves from the various pseudo-Buddhist sects. They have rightly defended themselves against being seen as a sect or a youth religion.

## ✸ Kalachakra Initiation

The Kalachakra Initiation, which the Dalai Lama has already celebrated twenty-five times since the 1970s, has caused a stir. Various Tibetan lamas have criticized the frequent and spectacular performance of this ritual. The term "Kalachakra" ("Wheel of Time") describes both a deity and tantric teachings. This involves the primordial Buddha (*Adibuddha*) who was born from himself and from whom everything that exists emerged. The Kalachakra is a component of tantric Buddhism, and its meaning is difficult to understand for the uninitiated. The performance of the rituals is intended to let the polarity of this world disappear and open a path into the formlessness of nirvana. This concept accommodates the longings of many Westerners who hope to overcome in this way the painfully experienced fragmentation in all areas of life.

Critical voices say that it is naive and unrealistic to believe that we can light-heartedly escape earthly hardships and enter into the bliss of nirvana with the fragrance of incense, some meditation, and a meat-free diet.

In addition, they say that various Tibetan lamas did not notice how little compatibility there is between the demanding Buddhist path, its ethics, and its sense of personal responsibility and the superficiality of Western media. This applies particularly to the various Hollywood stars whose commitment to Buddhism is not always free of vain self-promotion. "Buddhism Lite" can hardly liberate us from samsara, the troubles of this world. From the Buddhist perspective, pseudo-religiousness causes bad karma that does not lead to liberation but to sorrowful entanglement.

# ❀ You Shall Know Them by Their Fruits

Movements such as the New Age movement also frequently believe that they have found the answers to the
spiritual crisis of the West in the messages from the East.
Eastern spirituality and the attempt to develop a plane-
tary consciousness should lead to a spiritualization of the
"new humanity." People believe that they can leave behind them the superficial and empty world of consumers
(Buying makes you happy!) through this "new" deepened
and spiritualized worldview. The mechanistic worldview
influenced by Descartes and Newton should be replaced
by a holistic perspective. God becomes the life principle,
the primal energy of the cosmos.

Because people hope to find harmony and peace for the
entire world through meditation, concrete political commitment is often seen as unnecessary by this movement.
The growing environmental crisis is countered by a new
sense of unity with nature and the concept of a general
connectedness. New Age spirituality also likes to borrow
from Buddhism.

Considering the background of tremendous political,
economical, and ecological challenges, all these currents
are united by a minimal consciousness of the problems and
a lack of self-criticism. "We cannot avoid the crisis with

a reenchantment of the world and a collage of Far Eastern wisdom teachings, quantum physics, and meditation," writes Hans-Joachim Höhn.

The predecessor of many of these movements is Theosophy, which comes from the nineteenth century, and its founder, Helena P. Blavatsky. Her "Esoteric Buddhism" is a mixture of Christ, Lord Maitreya (the Buddha of the future), and the "Great White Brotherhood" for the coming Age of Aquarius. "All of these theories are wonderful, but the proof of whether they have truly helped a person or ultimately just serve that person's own egotism is shown only in the good works," is how Carl-Friedrich von Weizsäcker expressed it to the author.

## A "Buddhamania"?

France has been experiencing a veritable "Buddhamania." Even though François Jacquemart, publisher of a guide to Tibetan Buddhism, speaks of a maximum of ten thousand French Buddhists, other publications claim that six hundred thousand French have been seized by "Buddhamania." Even the Catholic Church appears to be concerned about this. Fashionable interest in Buddhism was triggered by the film *The Little Buddha* by Bernardo Bertolucci, which was apparently made with the blessings of the

Dalai Lama. In it, the director has portrayed the life of the Buddha in his own way.

Just before the premiere of the film, the Dalai Lama visited France. Much of the mass media, from the fashion magazines to the tabloids, focused on him and tried to market the Dalai Lama as part of the latest trend of Buddhism. Maybe fashion will soon also be inspired by a look at Tibet. The writer Jean-Louis Servant-Schreiber summarized his worldview in the following words: "This is my spirituality — a cocktail consisting of 'Buddhism Soft' and a pinch of humor."

## ❀ Love and Compassion

The Dalai Lama has repeatedly emphasized that he is not concerned with making the West Buddhist. He is convinced that Christianity will remain the religion of the West in the future. Many of the new religious movements can hardly expect a sympathetic response from the Dalai Lama, who may be committed to a dialogue among the religions but does not think much of a uniform and diffuse world religion. His political sense of responsibility toward the oppressed Tibetan people motivates him to participate in the troublesome business of politics. He is now considered one of the greatest Buddhist scholars of all time.

The Dalai Lama thinks that Westerners can especially learn from Buddhism and its many meditations to practice love and compassion, do harm to no one, and help other people. "We may be politicians, businesspeople, Communists, scientists, engineers, whatever — as soon as we have an effect on the society, the decisive factors are love and compassion. Each of us bears a responsibility for all of humanity."

## *Of Related Interest*

### Henri Nouwen
### LIFE OF THE BELOVED
*Spiritual Living in a Secular World*

"One day while walking on Columbus Avenue in New York City, Fred turned to me and said, 'Why don't you write something about the spiritual life for me and my friends?'

"Fred's question became more than the intriguing suggestion of a young New York intellectual. It became the plea that arose on all sides — wherever I was open to hear it. And, in the end, it became for me the most pertinent and the most urgent of all demands: 'Speak to us about God.'" — *From the Prologue*

0-8245-1184-0, $15.95 hardcover

crossroad

## *Of Related Interest*

### The Dalai Lama
### BUDDHA HEART, BUDDHA MIND
*Living the Four Noble Truths*

Is lasting contentment possible? Can we be truly happy? This book is comprised of passages from talks and essays given by the Dalai Lama and never before published in English. In them, he teaches that the state of the world and the state of our souls are deeply interconnected.

0-8245-1866-7, $19.95 paperback

Please support your local bookstore,
or call 1-800-707-0670 for Customer Service.

For a free catalog, write us at

THE CROSSROAD PUBLISHING COMPANY
16 Penn Plaza, 481 Eighth Avenue
New York, NY 10001

Visit our website at
*www.crossroadpublishing.com*
All prices subject to change.

crossroad